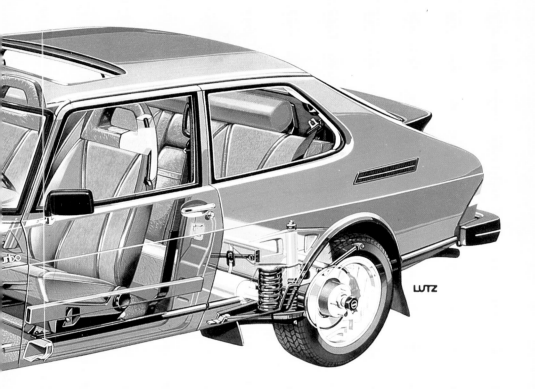

LUTZ

SAAB

THE INNOVATOR

MARK CHATTERTON

David & Charles
Newton Abbot   London   North Pomfret (Vt)

British Library Cataloguing in Publication Data

Chatterton, Mark
    The Saab
    1. Saab automobile
    I. Title
    629.22'22   TL215.S2

    ISBN 0-7153-7945-3

Typeset by ABM Typographics Ltd, Hull
and printed in Great Britain
by Redwood Burn Ltd, Trowbridge, Wilts.
for David & Charles (Publishers) Limited
Brunel House   Newton Abbot   Devon

Published in the United States of America
by David & Charles Inc.
North Pomfret Vermont 05053   USA

Contents

Preface

SAAB—Svenska Aeroplan AB—was formed in 1937, with private capital but on a government initiative, in order to produce military aircraft. The Swedish government thought, not without reason, that the political situation in Europe made some sort of military conflict inevitable in the near future. If Sweden were to maintain her neutrality and her independence she would need to be recognised as a state with a military force to be reckoned with. It was a logical step to begin to build up an air force—and to produce their own aircraft was essential. This new venture was based near the industrial town of Trollhattan in western Sweden. New offices and workshops were built just north of the city near the river which runs into the North Sea at Gothenburg—Göta Alv. As the Swedes had no experience of aircraft production they imported technical expertise from America: from Douglas, Fairchild, Boeing and others. Not unnaturally the first plane that they actually built—the Type 17—bore quite a considerable resemblance to the American planes of that era. This plane did not appear until 1940, and in the intervening period planes were being produced by Saab under licence from Germany and America. In 1939 the company expanded by purchasing the aircraft division of ASJ Svenska Järnvägsverkstäderna, whose premises were situated to the east of Trollhattan at Linkoping. The design and administrative departments moved to this new site.

With the outbreak of the European war the American technicians were recalled, which left the Swedes to do the final work on the plane single-handed. The Saab 17 emerged in the spring of 1940 as a two-seater, single-engined dive-bomber and reconnaissance aircraft. Just over two years later the Type 18 joined the range. This was a twin-engined reconnaissance/bomber which was available either as

7

the 18A with the 1,000 hp Swedish copies of the Pratt & Whitney engine, or the 18B with the 1,500 hp Daimler-Benz engines built under licence by Svenska Flygmoto AB. It was one of the world's fastest all-metal piston-engined bombers and remained in active service for fifteen years. In 1943 the Saab 21 appeared: it was a single-seater, and the only twin-boom aircraft with a pusher propeller to be built in any quantity during the war. It was one of the very first planes to be fitted with an ejector seat. After the war it provided Saab with a base for their first jet aircraft—the 2IR—powered by a De Havilland Goblin engine and first flight-tested in 1947. After the war aircraft production continued at Linkoping—and expanded into the civil field—with some considerable success.

1 Project 92

Aircraft production, and military aircraft production in particular, has always been a risky business. Often the supplier had to rely on just one customer—his own government. Aircraft being extremely expensive, the producer could never be sure of his future. Saab were very conscious of this, and in the early 1940s the management began to consider the production of other products as well as aircraft. At the time there was no problem about markets, but in the early 1940s the future was slightly unsure and prudence dictated that they examine all the possibilities open to them. The managing director, Sven Otterback, discussed what possible product they could use. Obviously it had to have some link with what they were already producing. There also had to be a demand for the product after the war, and preferably not too much domestic competition in the period in which they were establishing themselves. Prefabs, domestic appliances and the like were all given serious consideration, but all rejected. Saab really wanted to stay in the transport-production business. There was very little point in diversifying into motor-cycles or commercial vehicles as Husqvarna and Scania-Vabis already had these markets effectively covered. It was therefore decided to move into the production of cars. It was felt that after the war the pre-war trend of mass motoring would continue and that in the early years demand would not be met as both the German and British car factories would either have been bombed out of existence, or turned over to war products and take time to go back to car production again. Of course the Americans could be expected to come back fairly quickly, but many people doubted whether American cars had a future in Sweden anyway. The pre-war position had been that throughout the 1920s and 1930s American cars had sold better than

9

anything else in Sweden. It had been thought only they could stand up to the pounding given them by the awful Swedish roads. All the major American manufacturers had factories in Sweden assembling CKD kits. The only Swedish manufacturer at the time, Volvo, was assembling lightly disguised American cars. This situation persisted until 1939 when for the first time an Opel Olympia outsold all other cars, and the DKW had come up from almost nothing to feature high in the sales charts. Saab could see no reason why this trend should not continue after the war, and, if there were only small supplies of European cars available, there was an opportunity for Saab to penetrate the market fairly easily. The decision was therefore made to go into production of small cars.

The actual decision to put Project 92 into production came in the autumn of 1945—the car was known as 92 because the series 90 to 99 had been set aside for civilian production by Saab and 90 and 91 had already been reserved for civilian aircraft. In retrospect Saab were a rather unlikely firm to produce cars as they had no experience of anything other than aircraft.

Gunnar Ljungstrom and Sixten Sason

The first requirement was to get a design team together. The man put in charge of the team had no actual experience of car design, but had earned himself a reputation as a brilliant engineer. Gunnar Ljungstrom came from a family of well-known engineers—they take up their own section in the Swedish patent register. His grandfather had been a famous instrument maker; both his father and uncle had been inventors of considerable distinction; and three of his four brothers became engineers. He studied at the Royal Institute of Technology in Stockholm and graduated as a mechanical engineer in 1932. He then went to England to develop a mechanical automatic torque converter designed by his father. In 1936 he returned to Sweden where he worked designing engine accessories and in 1937 he joined Saab and was in charge of the wing structure design group until 1944 when he was put in charge of Project 92. He was given a team of fifteen draftsmen and engineers and pretty much of a free hand. The car which impressed him most was obviously the DKW, with its mechanical simplicity and front-wheel drive—it had a certain logic to it. There can be no doubt that this car was studied closely and the best features taken up to be used in Project 92— though it must be said that the design of the Saab was by no means a copy, as may be seen by the fact that the Saab 92 was significantly different in many respects from any DKW. On 5 February 1946 Gunnar Ljungstrom published a document entitled 'A short justification of production'—very valuable as it shows his thinking at the time.

The vehicle shall in relative price bracket correspond to the pre-war DKW, Ford's smaller models, Opel Olympia etc. The chosen design can immediately be characterised as a modernised DKW. The modernisation involves mainly: streamlined body shape (reduced drag), unitised body construction without separate frame (reduced weight), increased engine power (20%), softer springing, lowered centre of gravity with at least comparable ground clearance and headroom.

A streamlined body brings excessive length and weight. This project, however, reveals a car that is shorter and lighter than DKW, thanks to the following measures:

The engine is placed in front of the front axle, which has made it possible to place the driver's and front passenger's feet between the front wheels.

Furthermore, the rear passengers have been placed unusually low, which permits an elegant shape to the rear end of the roof. Weight saving has been achieved, partly by the elimination of the frame, partly by that the great loads from the wheels (in the spring mounts) have been conveyed into the body immediately in front of, respectively behind, the passenger compartment, whereby a minimum of material need be used.

It should be possible to increase the engine power somewhat without increasing the DKW engine dimensions by the adoption of slide feeding of the crankcase (applied in outboard marine engines since several years) and a cylinder head of light alloy. Both measures bring a small cost increase but need laboratory tests. Also other measures are investigated.

The electric starter motor and the generator are intended to be combined into one unit (dynastart) in the same way as in the DKW. Should it prove impossible to find a manufacturer of this unit, the engine can be made with a conventional starter and generator, which can be bought. This alternative is shown in draft 92.8005.

Softer springs can be chosen because, among other things, lighter unsprung parts are being used. Rim construction like Fiat's 15 in rims

11

reduce weight by around 2 kg per wheel. Torsion springs front and rear contribute at least as much.

Roll in cornering is counteracted by the low centre of gravity (appr. 10 cm lower than DKW). The centre of gravity has been lowered by placing the passengers in a low position, which in turn is made possible by the floorpan underside concurring with the car ground clearance.

The real contribution of Saab's aircraft building experience came with the use of unitary construction for the car. This brought them a tremendous number of advantages of strength, light-weight construction and all the benefits resulting from these. This, perhaps, represents one of Saab's great advantages over most of the rest of the motor industry. They were not afraid to use new ideas because they did not know what conventional wisdom considered right and what it considered wrong—they had no tradition resisting change. So in a way what was their greatest liability, their lack of experience, was also their greatest asset as it enabled them to take a logical approach to every problem.

One of the problems that faced the design team was the body. Some early sketches had been produced from within the team but they were rather heavy-handed and too much influenced by the outpourings of Detroit. Ljungstrom knew of a designer called Sixten Sason, and asked him to submit a design for a front-wheel-drive, four-to-five-seater car. This he did and his first design was accepted. Sason's training had been as one of a group of Swedish artists living in Paris. His father had been a stonemason sculptor. When he returned to Sweden, he served in the air force as a pilot and then joined Husqvarna. His sketches of motor-bikes got him a job in the design office. Unfortunately he had a crash in a military plane which put him into hospital for four years. In this time he studied engineering by correspondence, and when he came out of hospital he set up doing freelance design and illustration work. He was recognised as a brilliant illustrator, and quite an innovative designer —in 1934 he designed a transverse engine/gearbox layout which looked amazingly like that used on the Mini twenty-five years later. His car designs throughout the 1930s featured full-width bodies and unitary construction. Indeed Sason was remarkably proficient at all aspects of industrial design, and is a very underrated designer.

Sason's design was accepted in 1945 and immediately the sketch was translated into a small clay model. Above the waistline it was almost exactly like the production 92, but below the waistline it was cigar-shaped with a beak-like bonnet, faired wheel arches and a split rear window. A quarter-size wooden model, designated X9248, was then made, mainly for wind-tunnel testing. This showed the car to have a drag coefficient of 0·32, remarkably low even now. Meanwhile Sason and Ljungstrom were working on the construction of the car. They were greatly assisted by a scrapyard conveniently situated close to where they were working—this supplied them with ideas which they could not get from motor shows and suchlike, because they did not exist so soon after the war. The scrapyard also provided them with useful bits from which to make their first prototype. It was decided to make the car with a flat floorpan, feasible because of the absence of a transmission tunnel, and so give the maximum amount of space for passengers. The suspension was controversial, being independent torsion bars all round. Ljungstrom liked the idea of torsion bars as he felt that the system could be developed to give good handling and roadholding, whilst maintaining a comfortable ride. Steering was by rack and pinion; all other systems were considered inferior.

The Prototype

In 1946 the first full-size running prototype was built, designated 92001 and registered E 14783. This was exactly the same in styling terms as the wind-tunnel-testing model and it was all Saab with torsion-bar suspension and the rest of the features that were to appear on the production model. Though the engine and gearbox were DKW, and the petrol tank (mounted under the bonnet behind the engine) had the Auto Union linked circles in it. The car was tested for many thousands of miles, and was constantly modified. The most obvious modification was the alteration of frontal treatment—the faired-in headlights and rectangular gauze grille were replaced by more upright Volkswagen-like lights and a horizontally barred grille. Meanwhile Sason was working to improve the design of the car. 92001 looked very smart and advanced, but perhaps something a little less controversial might be better for the market. There were also practical problems with 92001; the doors were rather thick because of the profile of the side of the car, the faired wheel arches reduced drag but filled up with mud and snow and did not clear themselves. In the winter they would become so packed with snow that the car would become difficult to steer. Hence Sason made a prototype 92002 as a full-sized wooden mock up—narrower than 92001 and exactly like the eventual production 92. The car was painted black, polished with black shoe polish, and then placed on blocks beside 92001 and the two were compared. In practical terms the decision was already made, and 92002 was used as a master for the tooling. Three more prototypes were hand-made as replicas of 92002 and between them driven 200,000 miles for the final testing. They were constantly modified throughout their life.

Development

When it came to the choice of an engine for the new car there was very little discussion as to whether a two- or four-stroke should be used. It could be said that the engine was used purely because it was the type used by DKW. Whilst it is fair to say that Saab were greatly influenced by this fact, they would not have produced such an engine if it had in any way been unsuitable. The two-stroke had a great deal to recommend it to the design team. First, it was simple, important because Saab had no experience of car-engine manufacture and would have had many problems if they had tried to produce anything as complicated as a four-stroke engine. In addition to this, the two-stroke had far fewer parts. This meant it was cheaper to produce, particularly important with the great shortage of machine tools and materials at that time. Fewer moving parts also meant less wear, and so more engine reliability. The engine would also be very easy to service, and need less adjustment than conventional four-stroke units—an important consideration in a land of long distances. The two-stroke also has a high power output in relation to weight and displacement. It starts more readily at low temperatures and needs little warming up before full revs may be used.

The engine was of the same basic structure as that of the DKW, but it differed quite considerably in many respects—after all the DKW engine was a ten-year-old design. Much work was done on the inlet and exhaust ports to improve the flexibility of the engine and the smoothness of running. Engine timing was experimented with for similar reasons. Internally the main bearings were mainly of the roller type, but there was a double row of ball bearings at the rear of the engine. Small-end bearings were needle type, rather than the bushes used in the DKW. The carburettor was different from DKW's, and the exhaust system completely redesigned. The exhaust manifold was finned and ran across the front of the engine. The 'Dynastart' unit envisaged by Gunnar Ljungstrom was never actually fitted; it was decided that two separate units would be better because with a 'Dynastart' neither the dynamo nor starter were particularly efficient and to make a unit with the starter-motor power that Saab required would have entailed a very bulky 'Dynastart'. The dynamo was mounted on top of the gearbox, the drive having been taken through the gearbox. This was a very neat idea as it saved space around the engine—unfortunately the drive was taken off the end of the crankshaft by the device of one hexagon fitting within another and this used to work loose quite quickly. They also had early problems with sparking plugs: on two-stroke engines plugs get twice as much use as on the equivalent four-stroke. This, coupled with the high voltages needed to ignite the heavy petroil mixture caused a high incidence of plug failure. Considerable development work was done in co-operation with Porsche and the sparking-plug manufacturer Champion and eventually the problem was solved.

The very efficiency of the new car caused the Saab engineers some problems; people were finding that they could safely run the car throughout the winter instead of laying it up. Unfortunately the oils available at that time were not really suitable for such cold-weather running and Saab were finding that engines bench-tested on pure SAE 40 oil—being run at sub-zero temperatures and subsequently stored at a little above zero—were showing signs of extensive piston scoring and bearing corrosion. Similar tests run with an oil with suitable additives showed no such deterioration. All the oil companies in Sweden introduced a two-stroke oil with the proper additives, but when Saab began to export cars in any number, they introduced their own brand of two-stroke oil just to be sure.

The early cars tended to stall when freewheeling in extremely cold conditions and this caused the engineers considerable difficulty in discovering the cause. Rolf Mellde was driving a Saab in the 1950 Monte Carlo Rally, and noticed a distinct loss of power when

15

travelling uphill in a snowstorm. It was therefore concluded after much experimentation that the loss of power and stalling on free-wheel was due to carburettor icing. Ice formed in the carburettors from the air drawn in, and gradually blocked the jets—at first creating a venturi effect which manifested itself in the form of increased petrol consumption and loss of performance. The next stage would be the carburettor filling up with ice, which would, of course, stop the car. A hot spot somewhere in the inlet manifold might have helped a little but, being crossflow, no hot spot was available. It was therefore decided to attack the root of the problem and pre-heat the air entering the carburettor. A cowl was fitted to part of the exhaust manifold and from this cowl a pipe run to the air-cleaner inlet tube—this pipe being removable in the summer months. Hence all the air drawn into the air cleaner had to pass over the exhaust manifold and so was heated. Much winter testing in the north of Sweden took place to try to determine the amount of pre-heating that would give the best results—it was found that the worst times were when it was very cold with water crystals in the air, and when just over freezing in high humidity. In 1951 a removable pre-heater pipe was fitted to the production car—this made it the first car in Europe (and possibly the first in the world) to be fitted with such a device. It is interesting to note that very few cars are without one today.

For economy the car was not fitted with a water pump, but relied instead on a thermo-syphon system to circulate the water. This caused no problems in the winter but in the summer the car over-heated very quickly, and took a long time to cool down. Although the water jacket was large and the bore of the hoses extremely large, as may be seen in the cutaway diagram, the problem was not solved until the engine was changed and a water pump fitted.

The engine was fitted transversely in line with the gearbox so that on the right was the engine and the gearbox to the left. The ignition system was kept simple, consisting of a pair of coils. The radiator was mounted in a bulkhead behind the engine and fitted with a blind. Part of the radiator was blanked off to be used for the heater, which was mounted behind it. The actual size of the engine was 764 cc, 80 mm in bore and 76 mm in stroke. Compression ratio was 6·6:1, this giving 25 bhp at 3,800 rpm. The carburettor was a Solex 32 AIC downdraft, the petrol pump being mechanical. The pistons were flat top rather than the more old-fashioned deflector type—in fact they were slightly convex in shape. The combustion chambers were hemispherical.

The gearbox was entirely designed and produced by Saab, having no precedent elsewhere. It had three forward gears and reverse, with synchromesh between second and third gear. The gear ratios were 18·5, 8·55, 5·35 and 24·65 for reverse. The gearbox itself was very well made, as Saab used bearings where other companies used only bushes. The ratios were matched to the engine better than those of the DKW had been and so the car was quite brisk, especially in comparison with the rather sedate DKW. The clutch was a conventional single dry plate.

Meanwhile problems were being experienced on the production side of the operation. Svante Holm, the production manager, had the difficult job of converting part of the aircraft factory to build cars. Most of Saab's money came from the government and they watched what Saab did with it very carefully indeed. One of the big problems was the shortage of dollars and to make the bodies Saab needed heavy presses, available only from America. To buy them they had to get approval from the Swedish government who gave approval if the tools could also be used in the production of jet engines at the neighbouring Svenska Flygmotor plant. It is difficult to imagine how government officials became convinced that 500-ton presses could be used in aircraft production. However, convinced they were, and the press arrived, almost destroying the Trollhattan sluices when it passed over them and was found to have been packed upside down when opened at the factory! Another problem was the shortage of raw materials—especially steel. The suppliers could not supply their existing customers, and were very reluctant to take on new ones. Until they established their name (the early rally victories helped enormously here) Saab had a very hard time getting raw materials.

Volvo were developing a small car, and were rather ahead of Saab in their programme. So much so that quite early on they were taking firm orders for their cars at what seemed a very low price— only a little above Saab's projected cost price. This caused great dismay at Saab because they had very few ways of cutting costs—the back window was made smaller and the bootlid deleted in the hope of making their price competitive with Volvo. As it turned out, Volvo had wildly miscalculated and their price, when it was announced, was much higher than the one they had anticipated—and much higher than Saab's.

June 1947 was quite a significant month for Saab: the 92 was shown to the press for the first time. It received extensive press coverage and quite a lot of orders. The other significant event was that Saab acquired an agent to sell their cars. Philipsons imported cars to Sweden and assembled American CKD kits. They had looked at all the German manufacturers after the war and decided that it would probably take five to ten years before they got back to full production. So in order to have a small car to sell they started developing their own. They heard that Saab were developing a car and were interested. After they had seen the prototype they made an agreement to become the sole Swedish agents for the car. This suited Saab very well as it gave them a chain of outlets for their car throughout the country, which otherwise might have been rather difficult to come by. Philipsons also paid cash in advance for 8,000 cars, which came in very handy.

It was not until 1949 that the first run of cars were produced—the two intervening years being spent on final development of the car and of the factory. In the summer of that year a pilot run of about twenty-five cars was built—and production started in earnest, though hardly in bulk, at the end of that year. It is interesting to note that by the mid-1950s no American CKD kits were assembled in Sweden.

The Production Model

In December 1949 production of the Saab 92 began. Although the car was already known in Sweden, the prototype having been unveiled to the press in June 1947, it caused considerable interest—and excitement—amongst the many people who had placed orders. At this point it is probably helpful to describe the actual car that went into production. To begin with, it was green—saved all timewasting business of changing paints and the like. The car was described by *Motor* as having the 'low, sleek lines of a super-sports coupe'. Certainly the car was rather different from most production cars. From the bottom of the leading edge on the front wing to the bottom of the trailing edge on the rear wing there was one continuous and smooth line. The sides themselves were smoothly convex, broken only by the slight flaring above the relatively small wheel openings. The almost beak-like bonnet of Project 92001 had been flowed into the wider bonnet of the production model and was flanked by two lesser ridges culminating in vertical headlamps, the bonnet had been graced with a small central spine. Below and to the outer edge of the headlamps were small round sidelamps—the indicators being of the semaphore type placed high on the central pillar. The grille was placed low and was shallow, consisting of a gently curving opening running the full width of the bonnet with four horizontal bars across it. The bumpers were of a type that has come to be known as quarter bumpers, and extended well round on to the wings; they were fitted with overriders. Above the grille was a Saab badge. The roofline swept in an unbroken line from the bottom of the windscreen to the tail of the car. The windscreen was split, and below it was a small air scoop. The rear window was quite small and below it was the petrol filler, there being no external bootlid. The side windows followed the line of the roof, no quarterlights being needed. At the back was a small vertical section on which the rear lights and the number plate were mounted, the bumpers being similar to those at the front. The car certainly looked strange to contemporary eyes (as it does today), but it had a certain style about it, which represented a change from pre-war ideals, without falling into the American trap of producing the bulbous and ugly. The design needs no more justification than its exceptionally low drag factor, though it can also be said that it was a handsome motor car.

The interior was plain, though nicely finished in cloth. The dashboard was neat, the instruments being mounted in a long rectangular strip directly in front of the driver. These consisted of a strip speedometer, flanked by a fuel gauge, an ammeter and, on the De Luxe model, a clock and a water-temperature gauge. The De Luxe was also graced with a rear central armrest and an extra horn. To the right of the dash was a vertically mounted ashtray and an open glovebox. Centrally placed on the top of the dash was a rear-view mirror. The steering wheel was made entirely from plastic, including the spokes, which were horizontal when the wheels were straight ahead, and had finger spats moulded into them. Mechanically the car has already been described.

In their 1950 road test *Motor* were slightly puzzled by the car—it was rather different from anything that they had tested before and so they had nothing to compare it with. What surprised them particularly was the amount of power available from what was a very small engine in relation to body size. They obtained maximum-speed figures of around 65 mph, above average acceleration times and found that the car could be cruised for long periods near its maximum. They found that the best cruising speed for the car was about 50 mph, when wind, engine and road noise were very low. But it would cruise equally happily, although not so economically, at 60 mph. At 55 mph there was a certain amount of exhaust resonance. They were impressed with the fuel economy too: 'It will be observed that in the 30–40 mph range of steady speeds substantially more than 50 mpg is attainable, and an overall figure of 36·6 mpg was obtained in hilly country (with a fully laden car).' The delights of the gearbox impressed themselves on the testers: the combination of synchromesh on the top two gears and a freewheel making gear-changing a very simple business. The completely flat floor, with no transmission tunnel, was then a very rare feature. In addition to this a surprisingly large amount of interior space was available—the transverse engine took up little room (a fact that BMC discovered a decade later with the Mini). Space utilisation on the whole was very good—the full width of the car being available to the passenger compartment meant that the seats were the widest of any car in its class; this was enhanced by such things as the scolloping of the rear side panels to produce armrests. There can be little doubt that Saab's lack of motor-manufacturing experience, whilst it created certain problems, gave them a distinct advantage in many ways.

Of course the car was not perfect—agility was called for when loading the boot from the inside and even more when removing the spare wheel. Rearward vision was negligible, to put it kindly. The turning circle was rather large for a car of its size, and whilst road behaviour was generally very good the car could be provoked into doing some rather strange things at times, and it was very sensitive to the tyre pressures. Then there was the inconvenience of the starter cord which was regularly pulled off, and it was impossible to say that the car was overcooled. The pre-mixing of petrol and oil was inconvenient, but so was changing the oil on a four-stroke car. On the whole the faults of the car were far outweighed by its virtues.

The Early Years

The production figure for 1950 had been predicted at a hopeful 4,000. In fact because of various production difficulties only 1,246 car were made but 1951 was better with 2,179 cars. By the middle of 1952 only 5,300 had been produced—all green. In December a new model was introduced—the 92B: the most noticeable new features were the addition of an outside bootlid and the enlargement of the rear window. After all, the Volvo PV 444 had an externally opening boot and quite reasonable rear vision. Of course it is not entirely fair to attribute the redesign to copying from Volvo—the Saab designers were quite capable of recognising the deficiencies of their product—but equally it must be said that in an increasingly competitive home market neither manufacturer could fall behind in terms of quality or features. The addition of a bootlid necessitated the moving of the petrol tank to a position inside the rear left wing. Later when the Saab 93 appeared in 1955/56 it was again relocated between the wheels in space freed by the use of a U shaped beam. The battery was moved from the boot to a position under the bonnet. These changes made substantially more room in the boot, enhanced by the rear seat being easily removable to make the car into a 'semi-estate'. Other improvements included seat padding of foam rubber and curved front-seat back-rests.

The 1953 production figure of 3,424 was a step in the right direction, and in 1954 production made its largest jump to a figure of 5,138—the first time that production had exceeded the figure predicted for 1950. It was in 1954 that the last variation on the theme of the 92 was produced. The power of the engine was increased by 12 per cent to 28 bhp, an important change in line with the increased power of its competitors and a change that generally made the car pleasanter. The wheels received perforations to help brake cooling—and incidentally improve the appearance of the car. Bright metal strips were added above the wheel openings, which improved appearance and represented an early attempt at protecting the flanks of the car against accidental damage. The door windows received small clear perspex triangles across the top corner of the trailing edge. This was because Saab in fitting the car with its novel type of opening window had not realised that however little it was

21

wound down an intolerable draught blew around the rear passengers and hit the front-seat passenger (if it was the driver's window) on the back of the head. These ingenious pieces of perspex meant that the window could be wound down a little way to make the car interior less stuffy without great draughts entering the car. The trim materials were changed—the all-cloth layout was still available but was being superseded by a basically plastic layout with cloth inserts. These made the car look less plain, though some of the colour combinations, such as red and pale blue, were less than successful. Headlights and heater were improved and the small sidelights disappeared. For 1955 sales were 5,163.

Expansion

By this time it could be said that Saab were becoming an established make. The car gained a great deal of popularity within Sweden, and respect both there and abroad. Saab had eaten into the markets of both Volvo and foreign competitors—they could sell every car they made. In addition to this there was always the possibility of future export markets. What Saab badly needed was extra capacity—the Trollhattan factory was working at full capacity. Instead of expanding the Trollhattan factory, another factory was purchased in Gothenburg, a coastal town. Here it was decided that engines and gearboxes should be produced. This was rather a neat method of expansion as it enabled two rather different processes to be separated without breaking the production line. The purchase extended the shop-floor working area of the whole company to about 35,000 square metres. The Gothenburg plant was opened in January 1954, but no immediate production increases were possible because it took some time to restructure the Trollhattan plant—all was ready in the summer of 1955.

This was convenient, for the end of the 92 was at hand.

2 The 93

Gunnar Ljungstrom had never been pleased with the handling of the 92 with its oversteering characteristics and had wanted to change it at the earliest possible opportunity.

Suspension

A total rethink of the suspension, a very costly business, was needed. It was becoming more and more obvious that the car's performance was not really adequate—Saab were especially conscious that if they wished to export the car to America with a two-cylinder engine it would get the image of being a rather underpowered 'mini' car which was not at all the sort of image that Saab wanted to cultivate. Hence it was decided to bring together the development work that had been done over the years in a new model—the 93. It was decided to abandon independent torsion bars, and instead use more conventional coil springs. At the front independent coil springs were used. In order to improve handling these were made fairly firm. At the rear independent suspension was abandoned and coil springs—somewhat softer than the ones at the front in order to secure a good ride—were fitted to a U-shaped tubular axle, located by trailing arms and a central bearing. This slightly unusual rear axle was designed to keep unsprung weight as low as possible, and proved very effective at doing this. Track was increased by a little under 2 in and this caused the whole car to corner more stably.

The Three Cylinder

The two-cylinder engine was abandoned for a three-cylinder unit of similar but higher output—the engine being very much like the three-cylinder DKW unit.

The two-cylinder was by no means a bad engine—it provided the car with what was very brisk performance for its day. However, there were intrinsic problems which rather limited its life. To begin with, it was no more than acceptably smooth. It was also rather limited in its production of torque—and the range in which it was produced. The petrol consumption was rather poor with the engine stressed. One of the major reasons for this relates to the exhaust system of the car, and entails a little explanation of the theory controlling two-strokes.

It is desirable to maintain low pressure at the exhaust port during the middle part of the scavenging period, as without this effective scavenging would be impossible—in other words if the pressure were too high it would not allow the exhaust gases to escape properly. However, at the end of the scavenging phase, particularly during the period when the transfer port had closed, but the exhaust port remained open, it was desirable to maintain a high pressure at and around the exhaust port. This was to prevent the new charge being scavenged and maintains a high pressure at the start of the compression stroke. There are two basic methods of achieving this type of pressure sequence. First to have a separate pipe for each cylinder and having at a set distance down the pipe a bland or restriction which would reflect the exhaust pressure back, thus causing a pressure wave to reach the exhaust port at exactly the right moment. Obviously this system is rather bulky to use on a multi-cylinder car. In addition the system may only be tuned for rather a limited rev range as the bland remains static. The second system is to connect the exhaust ports by means of a suitable exhaust manifold. The length of the pipes between the different cylinders being calculated so that the pressure wave resulting from the opening of the exhaust port arrives just before closure of the exhaust port on the cylinder directly preceding it. This phenomenon is called 'pulse charging'. If it were applied to a two-cylinder engine the exhaust-port timing would need to be greater than 180°, thus making the engine completely unusable at low speeds. However, on a three-cylinder engine the timing could be 150–160°, giving an overlap of 30–40°. This meant that the ports could effectively be connected with relatively short pipes and, more importantly, that effectiveness would be consistent over a large rev range, thus maintaining good torque and specific fuel consumption over this range.

It was largely for this reason that a three-cylinder, in-line two-stroke engine was designed to replace the two-cylinder unit. At that time there was no discussion of a four-stroke engine, as Saab were still not in a position to design and build such a unit, and they seemed capable of producing a very effective two-stroke unit. To advise on the design Saab brought in a German expert. This is not to say that the engine was not designed by Saab: they knew enough about two-stroke engines to know exactly what they wanted and how to go about it, they merely recognised the wisdom of bringing in an acknowledged expert on the subject. The new cylinder block and lower half of the crankcase were cast in nickel alloy steel and machined together to ensure a good fit. The cylinder head was cast in light alloy and the crankshaft mounted entirely on single-row ball bearings, with the big-end bearings being double-row roller type. The small-end bearings remained of the needle type. Piston-ring-type seals were provided between the three crankcase compartments and at the flywheel end of the crankcase, which was sealed at the front by rubber gaskets on the two distributor gear covers. The crankshaft was fitted with a torsional vibration damper, which may be seen in the form of the large spring on the bottom pulley. The pistons were similar in shape to those of the two-cylinder engine, having convex tops. They were fitted with chrome-steel rings in order to reduce the high incidence of ring failure experienced with cast-iron rings. Probably the most interesting feature of the new engine was the combustion chamber. It remained hemispherical, as it had not been possible for Saab to find a more favourable shape. As may be seen from the two longitudinal sections the new chamber was rather different from the old one. To begin with, it was narrower at the base with a greater overall height, but the interesting part of the design was the section around the circumference of the chamber which left a gap of only ·04 inch with the piston at the top dead centre. This would compress a small amount of the mixture and force it into the main area of the combustion chamber and increased the velocity of the mixture. As a mixture heavy with oil was never as combustible as one without the oil, this made an enormous difference and significantly improved the performance of the engine, as well as making it smoother. An engine fitted with such a head would need a lower octane than one with a conventional head to obtain the same performance. At the time this idea was completely new.

The cooling problem was solved by fitting a water pump in unit with the dynamo. The radiator was enlarged, the heater getting its own heat exchanger rather than having to rely on part of the radiator. A thermostat was fitted into the top hose. The new front allowed more cooling air to circulate around the engine, and circular holes were added on the wheel arches behind the radiator at the points of low pressure to remove the air from under the bonnet—these were fitted with removable covers for the winter months. The radiator blind was moved from directly in front of the radiator to behind the grille at the front of the car in order to protect the engine.

The gearbox was new and thus the engine was now turned through 90° so that it was no longer transverse, the gearbox moving to a position behind the engine. The engine drove through the clutch into the gearbox, which was at the back of the casing, coming to the front of the casing again to the differential and so the drive shafts emerged from the front of the casing rather than from the back. The gear ratios were also different to suit the wider rev range of the new engine: 5·23, 8·53, 17·19 and 21·01 for reverse. The clutch remained largely unchanged.

The ignition system was rather more sophisticated, having a single coil mounted on the firewall and a distributor taking its drive from the front of the crankshaft rather than two coils mounted on the wheel arch of the two-cylinder engine. In order to reduce the risk of distributor flashover, caused by high ignition voltage demands, positive ventilation of the distributor was introduced with the advent of the 841 cc Saab 95/86. This consisted of a tube running from the air intake at the base of the windscreen to the distributor cap which was protected by a metal cowl. It was so designed that the air pressure into the distributor would increase as the speed of the car increased. The distributor was fitted with a rubber seal to prevent condensation seeping into the high-voltage section.

The exhaust manifold was of the 'pulse charging' type already mentioned, the carburettor being Solex 40 AI downdraft.

26

The three-cylinder engine showed itself to be a far better engine than the two-cylinder unit—smoother with more torque and a flatter torque curve. Certainly the car was faster through the gears, and would have been more economical had the extra power not been used. Even more power was required for the new 750 Granturismo. In pursuit of this the inlet, exhaust and transfer ports were cleaned up and polished and the compression ratio was raised from a nominal 7·3:1 to a nominal 9·8:1. This car was designed for road work, and for competition work further modifications were available. These were a twin-choke Solex 44 PII carburettor on a special inlet manifold with sports air filters and an extra fuel pump—making two SU electric instead of one. The car also had a modified front silencer and a larger-bore exhaust pipe. All this raised the power by about 20 per cent over the GT750 specification. The increase in the compression ratio brought to the fore another problem—the car had a certain tendency to blow cylinder-head gaskets. Under normal driving circumstances the problem was not great, but the extra load produced by competition driving was too much for the top end of the engine. There were a number of reasons for this: to begin with the cylinder head was made from aluminium, had only eight bolts to secure it, and the metal surrounding these bolts was rather thin. The engines were fitted with comparatively thick cylinder gaskets which had higher radial forces acting upon them than thin gaskets. Blowing the cylinder-head gasket in a Saab meant that the cylinder bores became covered with the glycol from the anti-freeze, and this decomposed the oil, thus risking the engine seizing. This glycol also had a similar effect on the gasket itself as it decreased its surface tension. Extensive tests were carried out on the gaskets in conjunction with a German gasket manufacturer—their method of testing various gasket alternatives is of some interest. The engine fitted with the relevant gasket was run up on the bench in the normal manner with methylene blue added to the coolant, already con-taining 50 per cent glycol. After the test the engine was stripped down and the gasket coated with chalk which showed up the methylene blue, and hence whether the gasket had blown. After much experimentation a gasket was introduced made of a closely meshed asbestos metal fabric, surface treated so that it showed a marked self-adhesion effect under pressure. It is interesting to note that the new gasket in terms of thickness was only about 50 per cent of the old one. This went part of the way to the solution of the problem, but it was not completely solved until the introduction of the 841 cc engine with its twelve-bolt cylinder head and more metal around the bolt holes to strengthen them. This engine was developed partly to solve the gasket problem and partly because it was felt more power was needed, especially for the 95. Obviously the main difference was the increase in bore from 66 mm to 70 mm. There was also a modified exhaust system with a more effective bland, and slightly altered exhaust timing—74 instead of 72. The induction system was also slightly modified. Although the compression ratio was unchanged, the larger bore resulted in increased crankcase compression, from 1:2·37 for the 750 to 1:1·4 for the 850. The modified engine had increased power and torque over the old engine, and it was coupled to two different gearboxes: the completely new four-speed gearbox on the 95 and the slightly altered three-speed unit on the 96. Ratios were 17·2:1, 8·5:1, 5·3:1 and 21:1 for reverse. The differential ratio was 5·43:1 on the 93, 95 and 96.

The Body

The car was given a new 'nose' to complete its new image and to make room for the new engine. The actual front of the car was flatter and the curves of the bonnet less pronounced, although the same basic shape was retained. The headlamps looked slightly recessed rather than slightly protruding. Dominating the front was a new grille—almost an upright rectangle, but tapering slightly towards the top, with the top rounded and the bottom corners also rounded; within this frame was a pattern of squares. The grille was constructed in two parts of cast aluminium. Flanking this grille below the headlights were two horizontal slots per side—these were finished with horizontal aluminium slats. The front wings were modified— the most obvious change being the larger wheel openings. The bumpers were new, front and back being of much heavier construction and full width. In design they were deep and flat-fronted and carried the normal overriders. Other changes included a water pump in the cooling system to try and solve the problem of inadequate cooling under certain conditions with the old thermo-syphon system. As no provision was made for a pump to be cast into the engine and compactness was required, the pump was put in unit with the dynamo so that it took the drive through the dynamo. Brake fade was reduced by improving the cooling of the brake drums—the front ones became finned. The fuel tank was moved to an even safer position and dashboard details redesigned—the instruments became rather smart with gold letters on a black background.

Production

The new model could top 70 mph, and acceleration from rest was better, although low-speed acceleration in top was inferior. Petrol consumption was also somewhat inferior—*Motor* obtained an overall figure of 32·4 mpg, and a touring figure of almost 40 mpg. It is fair to say that most of the problems of the 92 had been cured in the 93. 457 93s had been built by the end of 1955, production of the 92 not ending until 1956 when 680 were built. This meant the total of 92s was 20,128, 14,800 being 92Bs.

Saabs for Export

The possibility of exports was now seriously raised—before the advent of the 93 only about 5 per cent of Saabs had gone for export. With the combination of the new model and the expansion of the factory Saab had a suitable product to export and the spare capacity to produce it in sufficient quantities. America was chosen as the first major export market—it was recognised that there was a considerable demand for smaller European cars for the second car market, witness the success of the Volkswagen. There was also a demand for cars of sporting potential and in this respect the competition success of the car spoke for itself. The American market was better than the British because the cars needed no conversion to right-hand drive, and the Americans did not have that characteristic distrust of continental cars of the British. In respect of conversion for the American market very little was done, although such things as scuff guards on the rear wings and whitewall tyres were popular. In 1956 Saab established Saab Motors Inc in New York and in December of that year the first boatload of 250 cars arrived there. They were a considerable success, and the victory for Saab in the Great American Mountain Rally in 1956 provided a marvellous piece of advertising and greatly assisted early sales. In the first full year of sales some 1,400 cars were sold. The percentage of export sales was rising fast—in 1956 10 per cent of the cars were sold overseas, and in 1957 the figure was 20 per cent, of which 70 per cent went to America.

With this in mind it is probably true to say that many of the changes to the cars were influenced as much by the needs of the American market as by those of the home market. In 1958 the 93B was produced; this had a curved one-piece windscreen rather than the old split screen. With the advent of the new screen the car could be given more effective windscreen wipers—in fact they wiped a 43 per cent greater area than the old ones. The old semaphore trafficators also disappeared to be replaced by 'blinking' indicators—rectangular lamps placed low on the front wings, and also incorporated into the rear lamps. A great convenience was the incorporation of a self-mixing fuel tank, ending the need to have to pre-mix petrol and oil, except in very cold weather. In addition to this the percentage of oil in the petrol was reduced from 4 to 3. Safety-belt anchorage points were introduced for the front seats, and a very novel method of adjustment was introduced for the rear seat; a large wooden cam was placed under the seat and this could be easily turned to three different positions to alter the height, so that very tall people had sufficient headroom, or children could see out of the side windows. An anti-theft device was added to the car—the cable between the ignition switch and the coil was armoured so that it could not be tampered with. The rest of the electrics were improved as well.

The GT750

March 1958 saw the introduction of a new model to the Saab range—they were actually doubling their model line and running two models at once. It was obvious that the new model was primarily introduced because of pressure from America. It was the Granturismo 750—obviously Saab were delighted with the sales of their cars resulting from their competition success, but equally rather embarrassed by the fact that the 93, whilst not slow, was no sports car. It was therefore recognised that a faster Saab was desirable and as any plans to produce an open sports car had been scrapped, the car had to be based on the 93. Externally the car looked little different from the standard model—the strips on the wings were replaced by twin rubbing strips running down the bottom of the body between the wheel arches and ending in a scuff guard on the rear wing. The car also had a pair of chromed extra lights at the front. Inside the story was very different: the two front seats were superb, some of the best seats ever fitted to a production car. They were large, properly shaped, fully reclining, bucket seats, with additional pads on the backrest that could be moved up and down, the passenger seat having a headrest. The rear seat was very sparsely padded, and meant only for occasional use—the space beneath it being divided into three separate compartments for storage; under the armrest pads at the rear were bottle-shaped compartments. The car had carpets of a coarse hair variety. The instruments were more comprehensive than those of the standard car and consisted of a speedometer and matched round tachometer directly in front of the driver. These were flanked by fuel and temperature gauges. There was no glove box, but to the right of the panel a Halda Speedpilot and a grabhandle. The steering wheel was light alloy with a hardwood rim. The engine was basically the same as that of the 93, but compression ratio was increased to 9·8:1 from 7·3:1, and there were a number of other modifications. The gearbox remained as the three-speed unit until 1960 when the four-speed was introduced. The GT750 in 'standard' trim gave 45 bhp at 4,800 rpm, and 61 lb per ft torque at 3,500 rpm. This gave very good performance for the size of engine. Better performance could be obtained by converting the car to GT750 Super specification. The GT750 Super

31

was a very quick car indeed, although low-speed intractability and high levels of noise made it rather unsuitable for road use. All the high-compression 750 cc engines had one problem in common— a tendency to blow cylinder-head gaskets. This was unfortunate, but the eight-bolt cylinder head simply was not up to the increased compression. The problem was not cured until the twelve-bolt-head 850 cc engine was fitted some years later.

Formula Junior

The Saab competition and testing departments became interested in Formula Junior racing around the end of the 1950s. Management were also interested for a number of reasons: they thought that success in this field would boost their sporting image and so be good for sales; that some useful development might come from the project; and certain private individuals had been making Saab-powered specials to race in Formula Junior, and the management preferred competition to be with works-built cars. Management approval came with the proviso that the cars had to contain a high proportion of standard components and be front-wheel drive.

To be competitive the car needed a high power-to-weight ratio. It was calculated that the minimum weight would be 360 kg and the engine would have to produce 90–100 bhp in order to compete. Nobody knew if it was possible to have such high power with front-wheel drive; many suspected that handling would be so poor as to make it impossible to drive, or that all the initial traction would be lost in wheelspin. Obviously the project could not continue in such a state of uncertainty. It was therefore decided to lighten a 93 body and do the power-to-weight tests on this before going any further. This created further problems as it was calculated that even with a very much lightened 93 body about 135 bhp would be needed to give it the required power-to-weight ratio. Conveniently, a single 750 cc engine could be tuned to give 65–70 bhp, so it was decided that the only way out of the dilemma was to use two engines. The idea was not new—the 'straight eight' engine in the 300 series Mercedes was two four-cylinder engines linked together. The first attempt was in the form of two engines placed side by side and geared into a single gearbox casing. Not surprisingly this proved to be too much for the gearbox and so was abandoned. The engines were then put end to end, with the gearbox in the middle. It was found that with very little panel beating the engines could be put transversely across the car, with the gearbox in its normal position. A special casing had to be made and at the front of it was a pair of distributors. This arrangement gave 138 bhp, and propelled a lightened 93 body at speeds up to 122 mph. Obviously the front springs had to be uprated to deal with the extra weight. This was extensively tested and it was found to produce understeering, though to an acceptable degree, and a great deal of fun. Having discovered what they wanted to know from the car, which had come to be known as the 'monster', the linked engines were abandoned and work continued on the Formula Junior car itself.

The car had, of course, monoque construction in lightweight sheet steel, although the nose cone was fibreglass. Many parts were standard. The most significant non-standard items, other than such things as the controls and the petrol tank, were the engine and the rear suspension. The engine was an 841 cc unit bored out to give about 950 cc, mounted on its side to keep the profile of the car low. In front was a crossflow radiator without fan but with an internal pump. The pistons were new, of the bowl-in-head type, the flywheel was lightened and the clutch strengthened. Any problems with blowing cylinder-head gaskets were dealt with in advance by sealing with copper rings to each bolt. The exhaust system was modified and the ignition changed to triple coil. The neatest thing about the new engine was the carburation. Two twin-choke 40 mm Solex or Weber carburettors were taken and one was cut in half to leave just one choke. They were then mounted on to an inlet manifold in such a way that each cylinder was fed by one choke. The engine gave 96 bhp, the sort of figure aimed for. It was predicted that the car would have a problem with understeering, and in order to counter this the rear of the car was fitted with anti-roll bars in such a manner that the inner rear wheel could be provoked to lift, and the tail slide. This was a novel, but surprisingly effective way of taking bends. The cars had a fair amount of success in the 1961 season, driven mainly by Carl Magnus Skogh and Erik Carlsson. In June at Karlskoga they came fourth and fifth respectively, and in the next race Erik came first but the other car retired. At Canonlap there were cooling problems and both cars retired. In a Danish race Erik was seventh and Carl ninth. In September at Stockholm in the Swedish championship Carl was first and Erik second—they also set a new track record. The car was a very good straight-line car, but could not compete with the Lotus's cornering. At the end of the season the regulations for the next were published and it was discovered that the capacity limit was to be raised to 1,100 cc. As this would have made the Saabs completely uncompetitive, Formula Junior racing was dropped. Much had been learned from it though, especially about engine tuning. This would be used in the rally programme.

Rallying in the 1950s

Saab have been committed to rallying from the very beginning. In 1950, three weeks after the start of production, Rolf Mellde, at that time a company test driver, entered a car in the Swedish National Cup Rally, a very difficult winter rally, and won it outright. Greta Molander won the ladies prize. This created a lot of interest in the car. It brought orders in and it made raw materials' suppliers much more eager to deal with Saab. Saab never looked back because rallying had a further advantage: it provided the company with what came to be known as a 'rolling test bench'. In the early days money was somewhat short and rallying was seen as a cheap and very effective way of testing a car. In Scandinavia rallying is very popular—a higher proportion of people have competition licences than anywhere else in the world. One of the reasons for this is the fact that the roads in 1950 in Sweden were not very good—many not tarmac. So the similarity was strong between ordinary roads and rallying tracks and many Swedes were getting practice rallying almost every day. This worked in Saab's favour because in testing their cars in rallying conditions they were testing them in conditions very much like those in which the normal Saab owner would drive every day. There the similarity ended because the rally cars were driven much harder than even the Swedes drove their cars normally, so any weaknesses of design would show up very quickly and could be changed on production cars. In terms of long-term planning, the limits of, for instance, the handling may be seen in rallying when they might not be apparent in normal use. This was one of the reasons that independent torsion bars were not used on the 93. On the 92 it had been found that the car handled strangely near the limits of adhesion. This only showed up in rallying as the limits were far too high ever to be reached on the roads. Later on, rallying helped Saab to penetrate export markets—the American and the British markets being particularly good examples of this. This of course is the reason that Saab rally as near standard products as possible, for testing and so that people can know that the standard cars are tough. It is interesting to note that Saab have been constantly in works rallying longer than any other manufacturer, and that they are probably the only manufacturer to have entered competitions from the very beginning of production.

Sadly most of the records of Saab competition in the 1950s have been lost. They were the property of Philipsons and when the contract between the two companies was terminated in 1960 Philipsons kept all the documents and reports. A recent search for them has revealed nothing, and it seems likely that they no longer exist. This, coupled with the fact that the British motor magazines are reluctant even to admit to the existence of Saabs before 1960, let alone write reports on their performance, makes rallying information distinctly scarce.

In 1951 cars were entered in the Swedish National Cup again, though without quite the success of the previous year. However Greta Molander was first in the ladies class. She repeated this in the Rally to the Midnight Sun later that year. In 1953 Rolf Mellde and Greta Molander entered cars in the Monte Carlo Rally. Greta was first in the ladies class, although ninety-first across the line. Rolf was sixty-seventh across the line and won the Concours de Confort for cars under 1,100 cc. In the Rally to the Midnight Sun Saabs came first, second and third in their class, driven by Rolf Mellde, Greta Molander and B. Blomberg.

In 1953 Rolf Mellde won the Swedish cross-country championship outright, and was second in class in the Rally to the Midnight Sun. Meanwhile Greta Molander was winning the ladies classes in the Tulip Rally, the Rally to the Midnight Sun and the Viking Rally. Indeed that year she was ladies European rally champion. The Midnight Sun saw Erik Carlsson's rallying debut, as he acted as a co-driver on it. In 1954 hè had graduated to driving—Saabs of course, although not works cars—and won his class in the Swedish National Cup. In 1955 he was first overall in the same event. Greta Molander was first in the ladies class in the Tulip Rally. Rolf Mellde came second in his class.

In the 1956 Rally to the Midnight Sun Carl Magnus Skogh came first in class and Erik Carlsson was second. C. Coskul was first in the ladies class. In the Viking Rally Carl Magnus Skogh was first overall and Erik second. In the Wiesbaden Rally, a German event, B. Jonsson was first overall. Rolf Mellde was second overall in the Tour d'Europe Continental. In the Swedish National Cup Carl Magnus Skogh was first overall and Erik second. In Canada H. Blanchoud was first overall in the Gaspe Rally. In Sweden Saabs were entered in the Mobilgas Economy Rally: D. Persson was first in class, Rolf Mellde second, O. Lindkvist third and Gunnar Ljungstrom fourth. At the end of the year Saab made their American debut in the Great American Mountain Rally—a very tough event. This proved to be a very effective way of launching the car. It came first in the hands of R. Wehman, also won the team prize, the 750 cc class and the touring category. Suddenly, everyone in America wanted to know about Saabs.

In 1957 Carl Magnus Skogh was first in class in the Rally to the Midnight Sun and the Viking Rally. In the latter event Erik Carlsson was second in class. E. Roskuist won the ladies prize. Erik was first overall in the Rally of 1,000 Lakes. In the Swedish National Cup Carl Magnus Skogh was first overall and Erik second. R. Hopfen was first in class in both the Wiesbaden and Berlin Rallies. In the Acropolis Rally he was second in class, first in the class being H. Blanchoud, who was second overall. In the Adriatic Rally, R. Hopfen was first overall, and also won the European Rally Championship. C. Lohmander came first in his class in the Mille Miglia road race. H. Kronegarde was first in class in the Rally Atlas and Oasis in Morocco. In the Spanish National Motor Race they were first and second in class. There was no Monte Carlo Rally that year. 1957 was also notable for the fact that Erik Carlsson became a full-time employee of Saab.

In the 1958 Swedish Ice Racing Championship Carl Magnus Skogh was first in his class and Erik was second. Greta Molander was second in the ladies class in the Monte Carlo Rally, and first in the ladies class in the Sestriere Rally. In the Tliup Rally M. Kjerstadius was first in her class. In the Rally to the Midnight Sun Rolf Mellde was first in his class and A. Kilden was second; in the ladies class Greta Molander was first and E. Roskvist was second. In the Finnish Snow Rally C. Bremer was first overall, and in the Acropolis H. Blanchoud was first in class. In the Liège–Rome–Liège Moerculeoret and Hacquen came first and second in their class. In the Viking Rally Carl Magnus Skogh came first in his class, with S. Bjorklund coming second in that class and first in the ladies class. Erik came first in his class in the Rally of 1,000 Lakes. In the RAC Rally Kilden in a private Saab put up a very impressive performance, proving to the British journalists that there was more to rallying than Morris Minors and Standards—a taste of things to come. Saabs were first in their class in the Wiesbaden Rally, the Rally Bad Homburg and the Deutschland Rally. R. Smith was first overall in the Great Florida Rally.

The year 1959 opened with the Swedish Ice Racing Championships and Erik won his class in them. Meanwhile Homer Trotter scored an overall win in the Canadian International Winter Rally and R. Hopfen won the German Touring Car Championship. He was also first overall in the Wiesbaden Rally and first in his class in the Rally Bad Homburg. Erik came fifth overall in the Tulip with a clean sheet in his class and had the satisfaction of beating all the Porsches at the Zandvoort race. Greta Molander won the ladies award. Erik won outright the Rally to the Midnight Sun and Carl Magnus Skogh was second; Saab took second, third and fourth in the ladies class. Erik was first in class and second overall in both the Adriatic Rally and the Viking Rally. In the latter rally Olle Bromark was second in class and Greta Molander third. Erik was first in class in the Swedish Racing Championship and the Portugese Rally. In the Deutschland Rally he was first overall and fourth in the 1,000 Lakes —with Carl Magnus Skogh second and Olle Bromark fifth. Saab won the team award. It was obvious that Erik was having a very good season and he was competing with Paul Coltelloni for the European Rally Championship. It all hinged on the Iberian Rally: if Erik came fourth, or better, he would be champion. He finished second, but a trivial objection was put in about the colour of the numbers—Erik's car was dark so he had white numbers—the rules stated that numbers had to be black on a white background. Fifty points were knocked off, but 'as Erik would still have been champion another fifty was knocked off for the other door which put him down to fifth place and unfortunately cost him the championship. Saabs were also first in their class in the American International Rally and the Italian Mountain Grand Prix. In the Le Mans 24 Hour Race they were third in their class.

The First Estate

In 1958, for the 1959 model year, the 93B was improved slightly on a number of counts: the front seats may not have looked different from those of the previous year, but their backs were adjustable for rake. By means of a small lever and a notched cam, seven positions could be obtained. Windscreen washers were fitted which worked when the windscreen wiper switch was pulled towards the driver. Padded sunvisors were fitted, of a very safe type. The headlamps were improved, an asymmetric dipped-beam type being fitted. The glove compartment was given a locking lid and the aircleaner was improved. The 1959 model year saw a third car added to the Saab line-up. For some time it had been thought that an estate car was needed both for the home and export markets. However, the 93 bodyshell was basically rather an unlikely design to make into an estate car—there was hardly a firm edge on it anywhere and utility bodies do not usually lend themselves to flowing curves. A very reasonable compromise was reached by redesigning the body to the rear of the side doors and, instead of continuing the body's downward curve, continuing the line traced by the top and bottom of the door window along in a straight line. The tail was cut off sharply, though not vertically. The tops of the rear wings were allowed to continue slightly beyond the rest of the body to form slight fins. The rear pillar and the central pillar were almost parallel to the rear of the window frame. The rear lamps were paired one above the other and circular. The back bumper was based on that of the 93 but fitted closer to the body, extending further around the body sides and with the overriders framing the numberplate. The car had the interior trim of the 93, though the back seat had an arrangement by which it folded flat to accommodate extra luggage. In addition to

38

this the car had a third row of seats that faced rearwards. The two squabs for this neatly folded out of the luggage area floor—the backrest leaning against the rear-seat backrest. Due to the intrusion of the wheel arches the seat was not exceptionally wide but would accept two adults, if not in the same degree of comfort as in the rest of the car. In all a very novel and practical arrangement. Mechanically, however, the car was closer to the 96 model which it predated. The car had the 841 cc engine—the bore of the old engine had been increased from 66 mm to 70 mm, whilst the stroke had been left alone. The new engine produced 38 bhp at 4,250 rpm—5 bhp more than the old engine at an extra 50 rpm. However, increased power was not the only benefit of the new engine—the old eight-bolt cylinder head became a thing of the past and was replaced by a twelve-bolt head. The car also received Saab's first production four-speed gearbox, with synchromesh on all forward speeds. At the same time this gearbox, with rather different ratios, was fitted to the Granturismo 750. The early 95s were assembled at Linkoping.

Examination of Saab's production figures for the late 1950s show that they got their structure right. In 1956 5,640 cars were produced; in 1957 9,847 units; in 1958 13,968 and in 1959 17,778. The 93 was a great success, but if the success was to be maintained further progress was needed. The weak points of the 93 centred around the engine—the 95 had shown the way here—and the tail of the car was beginning to look rather old fashioned—it had been very little changed since the redesign in 1952.

3 The 96

Design Changes

The 96 represented another step on the way to improving the Saab design. The car was only redesigned around the tail; it is interesting to note that Saab redesigning exercises never involve both ends of the car at the same time—and it was the turn of the tail.
The car had to look different from the 93—but not too much so. Obviously Sixten Sason did the design work. The windscreen was enlarged by 117 per cent—wrapping around to the sides of the car.

The rear side windows were enlarged and reshaped. Between the rear window and the side windows were extractor vents for the new flow-through heating and ventilation system. The bootlid was enlarged and the catch moved to the rear skirt. The number plate was moved up to the bootlid and above this was a chrome handle to lift the bootlid, which also held the bulbs which illuminated the number plate. The rear wings were altered slightly in their design. The most noticeable aspect being the new and larger rear lights mounted high on their trailing edge.

The most important new feature of the car was the rear seat, widened by 10 in without increasing the external dimensions. This made it a true five-seater. The boot was also enlarged.

The fascia of the 96 was completely new. It was painted in the body colour, red, beige, blue or green, but it was topped with dark-grey safety padding and capped at each end with matching plastic mouldings. By the summer of 1960, wheels and fascia were changed to light grey, standard for all. The instrument panel itself was a dark-

40

grey aluminium casting containing a strip speedometer—with a fluorescent strip rather than a needle. Under this were four small round dials—water temperature, petrol, ammeter and clock. Initially the knobs were the cream ones from the 93, but they soon changed to dark grey.

On the right-hand-drive versions the front ash trays were a problem—the conversion made no provision for one on the fascia. The ash trays were therefore taken from one of the Saab planes and mounted on the door panels—early ones being like half a sphere, later ones more like half a barrel.

Obviously the engine was the same as that of the 95, and the only other noticeable change under the bonnet was the central bulkhead —which changed from plywood to steel. The car was introduced in 1960.

In October 1960 right-hand-drive Saabs were on show for the first time at the British Motor Show at Earls Court. Around this time the motoring press were allowed to borrow a couple of the prototype right-hand-drive Saab 96s for road testing. The prototypes differed from the actual production model only in detail: for example the door-locking arrangement was different. Most of the magazines had tested the 93 some years earlier, but as this model was never formally imported into Britain their opinions of it had been of little more than academic interest, although it is perhaps possible that the good reception of the 93 by the British testers influenced Saab when it came to the decision as to whether to export cars to Britain or not; as recently as 1958 *Motor* had tested a 93, and commented at the end of the report 'The fact that no arrangement for selling this car in Britain exists, although even the steel from which its structure is made is British, seems regrettable'—a clear message. For all that, the 1960 round of road tests took on a new relevance as the odd little car from the Land of the Midnight Sun was available for the first time to the British motorist. Without doubt the road tests were studied very carefully after Erik Carlsson's victory in the 1960 RAC Rally in November, especially by the sporting fraternity. In a way Saab were lucky as they could have had little better circumstances for the introduction of their car on the British market—amongst motoring experts the Saab already had a good reputation, and the 96 received universally good test reports in the press. The victory in the RAC Rally brought the car to the attention of the general public, and there can be little doubt that it significantly boosted the early sales of the car.

Autosport stated 'The two best features of the car are its road-holding and the exceptional silence of its cruising at speeds close to the maximum.' This view seemed to be generally held amongst the testers. *Motor Sport* said of its performance: 'This is not exactly GT performance but in the manner in which it corners and holds the road, and its vivid pickup in top gear, the Saab is a particularly pleasant car to drive.' *Motor* expanded on top-gear performance: 'The top gear acceleration in the 20–50 mph range is more of the order expected of a 2-litre "six".' Indeed a 30–50 mph time of 9·4 seconds in top gear was very good—rather better in fact than such sporting machinery as the twin-cam MGA and the AC Greyhound—it must be remembered, though, that the top-gear performance was bound to be impressive as top gear on a three-speed gearbox is normally rather lower than on a four-speed gearbox. In fact an identical Saab fitted with a four-speed gearbox recorded a 30–50 mph figure in top gear of 14·3 seconds. All the testers were impressed with the gearchange, though remarked, quite fairly, on the difficulty in engaging first gear. The heating and ventilation system came in for considerable praise, as did the space utilisation; indeed, more than one tester was so amazed at the size of the boot that he could not believe that the petrol tank had been fitted in under the boot floor ahead of the spare wheel, and so he placed it under the nearside rear wheel arch instead. Of course the car came in for criticism as well. All the testers were distinctly lukewarm about the visibility and criticised the car's relatively shallow windows and indistinct ex-tremities when viewed from the driver's seat. Saab could take small comfort in the fact that they did not receive so much criticism on this point as they had done over the 93 (and not nearly so much as over the 92). Some protests were also raised over what was felt to be rather a 'joggly' ride over certain rough surfaces, and the closeness of the window winder to the arm-rest, this tending to bruise knuckles. The general attitude of the testers towards the car is probably best summed up by the clasing remarks of the test in *Motor*: 'In short, this Saab 96 is not only a very sound and well thought out small car, but one which possesses both performance and charm to a degree that makes it easy to forgive its few foibles.'

Before leaving the world of road test reports it is worth taking a look at the question of petrol consumption. The fierce debate that tends to rage over the two-stroke figures is reflected in the discrepencies between the figures gained by the various magazines. *Motor* managed to obtain the best figure with a touring consumption of 43·5 mpg and an overall consumption of 32·2 mpg; on a fast cross-country run with the freewheel locked *Motor Sport* managed 32·8 mpg and with the freewheel in use they obtained 36·2 mpg. *Autocar* obtained figures between 28 and 30 mpg, whilst *Autosport* suggested that 30 mpg might be obtained with the freewheel in use. However, in February 1962 *Practical Motorist* obtained figures between 23 and 25·6 mpg. This to a great extent emphasises that the Saab is only an economical car if driven in a certain manner: if it is driven like a sports car—hard acceleration and hard braking—it will be very uneconomical. Naturally all cars will be uneconomical when driven this way but it is particularly the case with the two-stroke engine. This is why the freewheel only makes a limited difference to petrol economy as the gains of the periods when the car is freewheeling and the engine idling are largely offset by the fact that when the throttle is being used it is almost always for acceleration to a speed at which the car can be freewheeled again. The car is by a large margin at its most economical with constant speeds maintained with a light even pressure on the throttle. For example, at a constant 40 mph *Motor* obtained 50 mpg. So the disparity between the above figures is largely explained by the throttle sensitiveness of the two strokes when it comes to petrol consumption. Four–strokes may vary by over 10 or 20 per cent; in the same circumstances that of a two–stroke may vary by over 50 per cent. All the same, those readers of *Motor* who bought Saabs must have been rather disappointed with their petrol consumption.

The car cost £885 2s 6d, including purchase tax and import duty when it was introduced. This did not make it an expensive car, but it was still far from cheap—the Volkswagen de Luxe Saloon, probably the yardstick of small imported cars, could be bought for £716 10s 10d, and the fellow two-stroker, the DKW Junior could be bought for £799 17s 6d. In terms of home-produced cars the Riley One-point-Five cost £815 14s 2d. Even so the interest displayed at the Motor Show was encouraging. The actual figures for the British market in 1961 were 370, which while far from exceptional, was an encouraging start.

Saab-Ana

Towards the end of the 1950s Saab were becoming increasingly unhappy with their cars being marketed in Sweden by Philipsons. They did not think that the full sales potential of the car was being realised. One of the reasons for this was that Philipsons also marketed the DKW and so their interests were divided.

It was for this reason Saab bought ANA, who had assembled Plymouths and marketed a wide range of cars, including the Standard Vanguard. By 1960 they were in a poor financial condition. The company became Saab–ANA and started selling Saabs in September 1960, when the contract with Philipsons was terminated. Sales rose dramatically after this date.

The year was quite noteworthy for Saab's other models as well. Production of the 93 finally came to an end—in its last year of production it only accounted for 5,042 units of a total of about 26,000 units. The GT750 continued production with the 96 body. In order to remain in the under 750 cc competition class it retained the older engine. Though externally the car differed from the 96 in that instead of the chrome mouldings running along the bottom of the body from just behind the front wheel arches to finish in chrome cappings at the bottom of the leading edge of the rear wings. It also had chrome wheel rims, reversing lights, opening rear side windows in chrome frames and badges on the front wings proclaiming its superiority. The interior on the old GT750 had been so good that it was fitted to the new model with few modifications. The 93F, had its doors turned around so they hinged from the front. This was a logical move to bring the cars in line with the 96 and new GT750 models and also with modern European thinking that rear hinged doors were dangerous, as they could be caught by the wind and flung open when the car was travelling at speed. The 95 still had the 93B doors, hinged at the rear. This continued for some time, together with the 93 type fascia. Changeover to 96 type panel and front hinged doors for the 95 came in 1960 and 1961. The first 96 (Feb 1960) was called the 1961 Model, in order to justify that the 93F had been called the 1960 model.

The 1960 Rally Season

In the 1960 Monte Carlo Rally Saab entered a team consisting of Carl Bremer, Greta Molander and Erik Carlsson. All the cars managed to complete the rally, with Carl in ninth place overall and leading his class—Greta was sixteenth overall. In the Lyon–Charbonnières Erik was tenth overall, and second in the GT I classification. In this class he had a hard battle with an Alpine—he beat it at Solitude. However, later he lost his right steering lock and had to use a power slide technique to get round right-handers—using the hand brake to straighten up. Not surprisingly this lost him time and he could not quite beat the Alpine.

In the Tulip Erik and Carl Orrenius both completed the rally unpenalised and won their respective classes. Overall Carl was second and Erik was sixth. M. Kjerstadius was third in the ladies classification. Erik started very well in the Geneva Rally, but was forced to retire. In the Acropolis Erik drove well—remaining unpenalised—and won his class very easily, coming second overall. In the Austrian Alpine Erik was forced to retire on the Monza test with severe engine problems.

In the RAC Rally Erik completed the road section unpenalised. This was particularly good as he had two broken ribs from a previous rally. He proved to be completely uncatchable—except on the Brands Hatch circuit where he was beaten by the Minis. He easily came first overall, which was quite an achievement and ended the reputation he had for seldom finishing rallies. His car was completely undented, but after the rally when it was parked in London someone reversed into it and smashed the lights. The car made a star appearance at the Talk of the Town, rising through the stage on a lift—the car had not been washed, but Erik and his co-driver wore dinner jackets.

The Rally of the 1,000 Lakes proved to be something of a coup for Saab: Carl Bremer was first overall, Erik second and Carl Magnus Skogh was third—not surprisingly they also received the team prize. In the Finnish 500 Rally and the Finnish Snow Rally Carl Bremer came first overall, while in the latter Aaltonen came second in another Saab. Carl Magnus Skogh won the Rally to the Midnight Sun, the Swedish Rally and the Viking Rally. Carl Bremer was first in his class and second overall in the Polish Rally. Homer Trotter was first in his class in the Canadian Winter Rally. Saab also did well in endurance races. They were first in class in the Spanish National Motor Race, the Nürnberg 6-Hour Race and the American Lime Rock Little Le Mans.

In the spring of 1961 further changes were made to the 95: the 93 type instruments were replaced by those from the 96, the chrome cappings to the rear pillars were deleted and an aerofoli was added to the back of the roof of the car. This aerofoil, in simple terms, consisted of a slot running the width of the back window $4\frac{1}{2}$ in in from the trailing edge of the roof, the slot itself being $1\frac{1}{2}$ in wide. This created a downward flow of air over the back window instead of the upward flow more normal in estate cars. In this way it cured the problem of the rear window fouling up—a problem that many other manufacturers have only recently admitted having by their fitting of rear washers and wipers to their estate cars and hatchbacks. Other less significant changes made to the whole range of cars in 1961 included new colours, new upholstery, longer mudguards, electric clock and grey wheels. A delivery van based on the 95 was introduced on the Danish market.

The 1961 Rally Season

Erik entered the 1961 Monte in a 95 estate car with a four-speed gearbox. Everyone foresaw that Panhard was in a good position to win the rally, which they did, although Erik was proclaimed by many as the moral winner although placed fourth overall. In the Tulip Saab did quite well, with Carl Magnus Skogh coming third overall and first in class; Saabs also came second and third in class. Erik started well, but did not manage to complete the rally. He made up for this by his performance in the Acropolis when he scored a very convincing win over the rest of the field.

In the Rally to the Midnight Sun Carl Magnus Skogh was first and other Saabs were third and fourth. In Class 1 (unmodified cars up to 850 cc) Saabs came first, second, third and fourth. In Class 8 (as Class 1 but modified) they came first, second, third, fourth, fifth and sixth. Pat Moss was second in the ladies class in a Saab. Erik completely wrote off his car—he came round a corner and was suddenly confronted by a non-competing Volvo on the wrong side of the road and that was it. Both driver and co-driver walked away unhurt. In the Austrian Alpine Erik's car refused to start because of engine failure.

In the Liège–Sofia–Liège Erik was doing very well in the early stages, beating all the small cars and many of the big ones too. Unfortunately he was forced to retire with piston failure. In the RAC Erik drove immaculately again to win for the second time in succession. Two other Saabs were entered but experienced reliability problems, one having to retire.

Saab were also first overall in the Canadian Winter Rally, the Finnish Snow, the Norwegian Winter and the Nordic Championship. In the Polish they were second overall and in the Rally of the 1,000 Lakes they were fourth. This rally was also notable because it was Pat Moss's first drive in a Saab. She was doing very well but was a bit confused by taking a left-hander in a left-hand-drive car instead of her more normal right-hand-drive. She hit a bank quite fast and rolled two or three times. The car started but she had to retire because the front bumper had jammed a front wheel and was of such a heavy gauge that it could not be bent back. The car was later thrown into a lake.

The GT850

In 1962 the GT750 was replaced by the GT850, which came to be known as the Saab Sport on the European market and the Monte Carlo 850 on the American. Obviously the Sport had the 841 cc engine fitted, but it was radically different from the 96 engine: it produced 52 bhp with the aid of triple carburettors. However, the most significant change was in lubrication. Instead of retaining the petroil system of the other Saabs, with the attendant problems of inadequate closed-throttle lubrication, Saab had fitted the engine with a separate lubrication system. This consisted of a tank under the bonnet from which oil was pressure fed to the bearings and the cylinders. This was the first production Saab to be fitted with front disc brakes and is considered in greater detail later.

The 1962 Rally Season

There can be little to say about Erik's performance in the 1962 Monte: very good and very consistent. The car itself ran perfectly and Carlsson won most of the stages and the rally itself. This was a quite remarkable achievement as the Monte Carlo Rally had always favoured big, powerful cars (preference given to those of French origin) and the small cars had always been consigned to battle it out for places in the classes. Saab's winning a Monte turned this tradition upside down and opened a new era. On the Monaco circuit at the end of the rally—totally unsuited to the Saab—Erik managed an excellent fifteenth. Carl Magnus Skogh came sixteenth overall and, of ten Saabs that started, six finished.

One of Erik's prizes was a free entry to the East Africa Safari—he had already won one entry as part of his prize for winning the RAC so he gave the second to Pat Moss. She used her newly bought and converted 96, on the understanding that after the rally Saab would restore it to pre-rally condition. Around that time there were pictures of Pat rolling her Saab on the cover of *Life* magazine. This had happened before the start of the rally when Pat and Erik were asked to help the photographers to get some good shots. This they did at an old autocross course. However, Pat hit a hidden ditch and rolled—much to the delight of the photographers. Luckily the car was only lightly damaged. At the halfway stage Pat was well up with the leaders, the car having been completely reliable except for losing the self-centring action on one steering lock. Erik's was not so reliable and he was well behind the girls. The entertainment began on the second half of the rally when on a night section a buck jumped on to the bonnet of Pat's car. It did considerable damage—she had only one light left and the car's distributor cap had been smashed. This was replaced, but it was found that the fan belt pulley was bent. By some remarkable coincidence Erik turned up, and he just happened to have a fan belt pulley on him. This was fitted and they continued. They made up the lost time very well and were

Thirty years of Saab cars – from a 1980 Saab Turbo to Project 92001.

Suspension layout—remaining basically unchanged for all two stroke and V4 saloons past 1956. Note U-shaped back axle.

From left to right: Svante Holm, Tryggve Holm, Gunnar Ljungstrom, Sixten Sason and Rolfe Mellde.

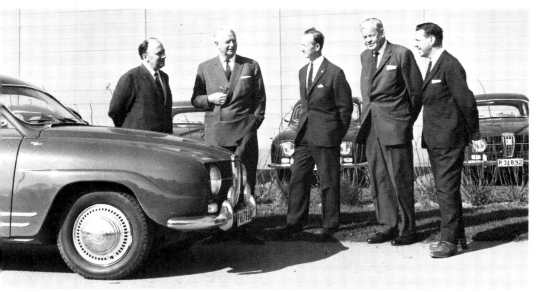

Some early ideas for Project 92, the upper two showing American ideas.

A model of the Saab 92001.

The first full-size running prototype, the 92001 designed by Sixten Sason. Saab's aircraft building experience gave them a number of advantages in the building of the car— its strength, lightweight construction and low drag co-efficient.

Original drawings of the Saab 92.

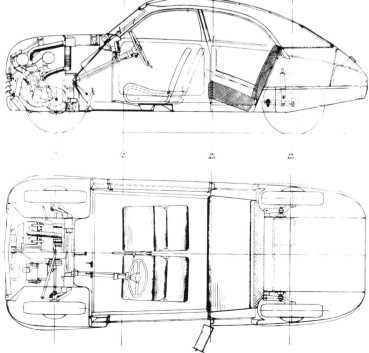

A wooden mock-up of the Saab 92.

The production model of the Saab 92, introduced in December 1949. *Motor* described it as having the 'low, sleek lines of a super-sports coupé'. It was certainly rather different from most production cars. From the bottom of the leading edge on the front wing to the bottom of the trailing edge on the rear wing, there was one continuous and smooth line.

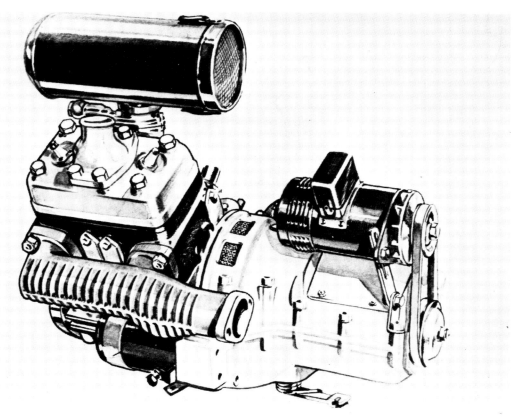

The original Saab 92 engine and gearbox.

The Saab 92B with ventilated wheels and rubbing strips.

Rear view of the Saab external boot lid and enlarged rear window.

The 1956 Saab 93.

Part of the Saab 93 production line.

The interior of the Saab 93 fitted with Saxomat clutch.

Gunnar Ljungstrom, the man put in charge of the team that developed and designed the 92, shown here with the 93.

The first Saab estate car, produced in 1959.

The 1960 Saab 96. The car was designed at the tail with a larger rear window, boot and more passenger room in the rear seats.

The 1965 Saab Sport with the completely redesigned front end.

The 1965 Saab 95.

The Saab 96 V4 engine compartment.

The final form of the Saab 96.

The final form of the Saab 95.

The Saab 92.

A pair of Saab 92s in an early event.

The first international rally for the Saab 92. In the early days rallying was an advantage to Saab in that it provided them with a 'rolling test bench'. With limited finances, rallying was seen as a cheap and very effective way of testing a car. In Scandinavia rallying is a very popular sport, and there is a higher proportion of people holding competition licences than anywhere else in the world. One of the reasons for this being that the roads were not very good—many not in tarmac.

The Saab Sonett Super Sport in competition; designed by Rolfe Mellde, it was based on the 93. It was first seen at the Stockholm Motor Show in 1956 and was not for sale.

Saab 93s racing against D.K.Ws.

Linked engines for the 'Monster'.

The Saab Formula junior car. The car was constructed of lightweight sheet steel. The engine was an 841 cc unit bored out to give about 950 cc, mounted on its side to keep the profile of the car low, producing 96 b.h.p. The cars had a fair amount of success in the 1961 season, driven mainly by Erik Carlsson and Carl Magnus Skogh.

Erik Carlsson and Gunnar Palm in the Rally to the Midnight Sun in which they gained second overall.

A rare competition outing for the Saab Sonett II in the 1966 Coupe des Alpes driven by Eric Carlsson with navigator Torsten Aman.

Erik Carlsson driving to victory in the 1963 Monte Carlo Rally, scoring his second consecutive victory.

highly placed at the finish. One of the tests was for the brakes on a Tapley meter. Pat had not come across one of these before and braked in a normal fashion without the jerk needed for a good reading. The resulting figure dropped her to third place—which she was not pleased about. Coupled with this, everyone thought she had run out of road and nobody believed that she had been jumped on by a buck. Erik had almost no brakes at the end of the rally, but managed to get an excellent figure on the Tapley metter by jamming the car into first gear at the relevant moment!

In the Tulip Erik was third overall. Pieterman retired after rolling his car and Carl Magnus Skogh had to retire on the penultimate stage after crashing his. On the Acropolis Damascos was the first retirement when early in the rally he crashed and broke his arm. Carl Magnus Skogh retired with disc failure and a locally entered Saab broke its crankshaft. Erik drove hard and came second overall—very close to the leader. In the Polish Rally Erik retired after rolling his car on a tricky right-hander. In the German Erik came sixth overall, but the event seemed as much a road race as a rally and was not really suited to the Saab.

In the Geneva Rally Erik came second, just ahead of Pat, the two having competed very hard. This should have made Erik the European Rally Champion, but as not enough people had entered the Geneva Rally for it to count he had to be content with being runner-up—this was a great disappointment, but a moral victory. In the RAC Erik again proved himself unbeatable by sheer good driving—he won the event and most of the stages. This was completely unprecedented for one man or for one marque to win the rally three times in a row. There is a story that on a special stage Erik was put off course mid-corner by a bump, hit a bank, did a somersault in mid-air, and landed on his wheels, still motoring. Erik denies it.

Saab also gained overall thirds in the Rally to the Midnight Sun and the 1,000 Lakes Rally.

In 1962 a total of 35,890 Saab cars were manufactured, just under 10 per cent of these being 95s, and Saab's share of the Swedish market had risen to 12·8 per cent against 11·4 the previous year and 6 per cent in 1959, before the introduction of the 96. British sales were remarkably good, rising to 1,009 in 1962 from the previous year's figure of 370. The following year sales rose again to 1,358. Obviously the fact that the first continental car to win a post-war RAC Rally was a Saab, which won it three times in a row, was having some effect on the car-buying British public.

The 1963 Model

The most noticeable difference in the 1963 car, introduced in October 1962, from the 1962 was the change from a separate Saab badge over the grille, to one cast into the grille. This improved the look of the front considerably, and also served to dispel the rumour that the grille was made of chicken wire. Other changes included the incorporation of a half horn ring on the 95 and 96 models, the fitting of a larger interior mirror and slightly modified heating and ventilation. The Saab Sport received a new instrument panel based on the fascia of the 96 instead of that of the 93, basically merely a regrouping of the existing instruments. The most noticeable change was the movement of the two smaller instruments, the fuel and temperature gauges, from positions flanking the two major instruments to positions between them, thus making the actual instrument cluster rather more compact and easily read. The other notable feature was the deletion of the Halda Speedpilot as standard equipment: obviously the car was being aimed more at the fast tourer market than at the competition market, though a Speedpilot was still a listed extra.

It was in 1963 that a four-speed gearbox was offered on the 96 as an option on certain markets, the three-speed gearbox remained as the standard fitment, and the only one available on the home market. The gear ratios and the final-drive ratio were exactly the same as those on the 95, except for top gear which was marginally lower at 4·61:1 on the 96 as against 4·5:1 on the 95. The four-speed gearbox gave the 96 a slightly higher top speed than its three-speed counterpart, and slightly better petrol consumption. The acceleration from the rest was rather slower, because of the extra gear changing involved, and top gear acceleration was grossly inferior. Overall, the four-speed gearbox made the 96 a rather more flexible car as the extra ratio enabled drivers to keep within the rather limited usable rev range for a greater proportion of their driving time. The extra £42 it cost in Britain was probably worth it, if only for the synchromesh on first gear—no longer would the 96 owner have to face the terrible grinding that accompanied a less than perfect change to first on the three-speed gearbox. However, it must be said in defence of the three-speed gearbox that it had a delightful positiveness rather lacking in the four-speed unit.

The 1963 Rally Season

The conditions in the 1963 Monte Carlo were ideal for Saab, and Erik was much fancied to repeat his previous year's win, although the competition was probably even stronger. However, he drove immaculately throughout the rally and scored his second consecutive victory. In the Canadian Winter Rally Homer Trotter was fifth overall. Erik had the only works Saab in the East Africa Safari. He made a very good start, leading for the entire northern loop and half of the southern loop—three-quarters of the rally. Unfortunately he had a collision with a very solid ant-bear which pushed the anti-roll bar into the drive-shaft universal joint, causing him to retire.

Saab were rather unfortunate in the Acropolis. First Erik went off the road on a fast right-hander and hit a bridge. This broke a front wishbone, and he had to retire. Then Olle Dahl rolled his car and in the process knocked down two trees and wrote off the car—he escaped uninjured. The Austrian Alpine was little better. Erik first lost a considerable amount of time—collecting more than a few time penalties—with what was described as a slight navigational error. He was then forced to retire with a broken piston. In the Marathon de la Route Erik came second.

Simo Lampinen was second overall in the Rally of the 1,000 Lakes. In the Shenstone Rally Pat, partnered by David Stone, was second overall. Bad luck struck early in the RAC Rally. Gilmo's Saab fell off the jack whilst having its wheels changed prior to the pre-rally scrutineering. The car was so badly damaged that it could not start the rally. Erik drove consistently well throughout and finished third, first in his class. Olle Dahl was eleventh, second in class and Ake Andersson was twelfth. Another Saab had the misfortune to roll down a soft bank and lodged against a tree—oddly neither car nor crew were badly damaged.

In 1963 Saab also gained an overall second in the Finnish Snow Rally, the Rally to the Midnight Sun and the Spa–Sofia–Liège. They were third in the Norwegian Winter Rally and first in the Rally Vltava.

The 1964 Model

The 1964 Saabs were introduced in September 1963. From the outside they could be distinguished from a 1963 model by the addition of a rather large Saab badge on the boot, or tailgate. This meant that from whichever angle the car was viewed, there could be no doubt that it was a Saab: on the 96 it was stated in no less than eight places. However, more beneficial improvements were made to the 1964 model. The handbrake was changed so that it worked further up on the rack—when it was on it was almost vertical, and when fully off at an angle of about 45°. It looked a little strange but, with no transmission tunnel to mount it on, this was the best way of bringing it within easy reach of the driver. The old system, which had the handbrake right on the floor when fully off, was unacceptable because the handbrake was also quite well forward. This made it difficult to use in normal circumstances and almost impossible in an emergency with the driver wearing a seatbelt. The windscreens fitted to the 95s and 96s had a safety impact zone, and that fitted to the Sport was laminated. In America the Monte Carlo 850 was renamed the Gran Turismo 850. All cars with four-speed gearboxes were fitted with an anti-theft device which meant that the ignition key could not be removed unless the gear lever was in reverse. In theory this was a far better idea than the steering lock, as it meant that the possibility of the car being rolled down a hill with the steering locked, and thus being involved in an accident, was removed. So the car was safe, and fiendishly hard to steal. However, reverse did not always engage very readily with the car stationary, and even if it could be engaged, the key did not always come out very easily. It got to be so much of a problem that Saab GB had to approve a modification to remove the device. The instrument panel of the 95 and 96 was redesigned. This gave it a totally new look, in keeping with the general move away from the strangely shaped instruments of the 1950s. The new instruments consisted of a large round speedometer directly in front of the driver, flanked by two smaller instruments—though not as small as in the previous dash. These were the water temperature and petrol gauges. A matching clock was placed in the centre of the fascia, so that it could not be confused with the more important instruments and it was also easier for the passenger to read. The tops of all the gauges were at the same height. The ammeter had been deleted, replaced by a charge indicator which glowed orange when the dynamo was not charging and adjusted not to light up with the car freewheeling. A second indicator repeat lamp was added so that each side had its own lamp. Other than a redesigned front ashtray the rest of the controls remained largely unchanged. Opinions of the newer instrument panel vary; certainly it was safer than the old one in that the instruments were larger, clearer and arranged so that there could be no confusion over which was which. Most important, they were all in a single plane, so could be read more quickly, requiring only one glance to see them all. The old instruments were on two separate vertical planes with the bottom row of four matched; the brightly coloured gauges certainly needed more than a passing glance to glean the required information. Certainly the new instruments were an example of clarity, but to some eyes they were rather dull compared with the old ones—indeed on their painted fascia they looked almost utilitarian. However, all the road testers of *Motor* approved.

The most important innovation for 1964 came in braking. Saab became the first manufacturer to develop and introduce a diagonally split braking system. Unusual because in 1964 safety features did not sell many cars and in the short term it was impossible to recoup the production and development costs of such a project. It is therefore obvious that Saab were not introducing it as a gimmick to boost sales, but as a genuine attempt to build a safer car. In retrospect it may be seen that Saab's long sightedness paid off because split-circuit brakes are now fitted to most cars, and diagonally split circuits are acknowledged to be the best. The system consists of two separate braking circuits coming from a common master cylinder. Each circuit acts upon one front wheel and the rear wheel diagonally opposite to it. In this way, if a brake pipe or hose becomes damaged, the driver will not lose his hydraulic braking power completely as he would on a car with single-circuit brakes, but will retain half of his system in operation. With diagonally split brakes the risk of the wheels locking and the car getting into a skid is reduced, and there is more balanced braking in emergency. General braking was improved by the fitting of Lockheed self-adjusting drum brakes at the front. These were fitted to keep the front brakes constantly at their most efficient point of adjustment.

The 1964 Rally Season

The 1964 Monte Carolo Rally was mainly noted at the time for the fact that Ford of America, after having come so close to winning in 1963, tried to move in in a big way with a vast budget and a number of top drivers. As significant for Saab, and probably more significant in the long run, was the fact that BMC had replaced the Mini Coopers used in 1963 with the appreciably more competitive Cooper S. Taking this into consideration, Saab did not expect to add a third victory to those of 1962 and 1963. Also against Saab was the almost complete absence of snow and ice that had characterised the 1963 event, and the change from the mountain circuit at the end of the rally to a race around the Monaco Grand Prix circuit, to be run without handicap, thus favouring the bigger, more powerful cars. The two Saab Sports of Erik Carlsson and Pat Moss (it was Pat's first drive as a member of the Saab team) started from Oslo and went well throughout the rally. However, because of their relative lack of power they did not put up particularly good showings in the tests. The first two were very fast and were easily won by Ljungfeldt in a Ford Falcon with the Saabs out of the first eight. The third test, supposedly primarily a small-car test, was again won by the Falcon, with the Saabs only managing 6th and 8th places—mainly due to the Coopers. The fourth test was a sports-car test, won again by the Falcon. In the fifth and last test about 20 per cent of the 23 km was covered in ice. Here the Saabs really came into their own for the first time in the event and Erik Carlsson took his Saab into second place, behind Ljungfeldt's Falcon, and Pat Moss took hers to fifth. When the preliminary (pre-circuit race) classification was published it showed that Hopkirk in a Cooper S was leading by 31 sec from Erik Carlsson with Pat Moss third, 18 sec behind Erik. The amazing

Ljungfeldt was lying fifth and needed to make up 33 sec to come second and 64 sec to win. In the event he made up 40 sec on Erik, so the Saabs had to be satisfied with 3rd and 5th positions overall, with Pat Moss gaining a comfortable victory in the Coupe des Dames. This good overall performance pleased Saab, but served to emphasise the fact that the car was made less competitive than it might have been by its relatively low power-to-weight ratio compared with the Copper S Minis. The result must also have been disappointing for Erik, deprived of his third consecutive win in the Monte.

The next rally—the Italian Rally of the Flowers—provided an excellent result for Saab, with Erik gaining first place and Pat second; the gravel roads, difficult passes and snow suited the Saabs very well. Immediately after the 'Flowers' came the East Africa Safari, with the Saabs tipped as hot favourites because of Erik Carlsson's fantastic performance in 1963. Sadly the Saabs did not win but it could be said that they had the last laugh. One of the problems they faced was the large stretches of water that covered the route in places—the electrics on the two-stroke Saabs are somewhat vulnerable to flooding, especially the distributor, placed just behind the front grille. Pat Moss's car suffered badly in this way, and she lost a lot of time because of it. Indeed, she almost retired from the rally after having removed a plug and found the cylinder full of water. It was only because nobody came to pick her up that she tried to start the car, after over an hour, and found that she was able to continue, albeit with something of a drop in performance. She finished in ninth position overall, which was remarkable considering the setbacks she had faced. From the start of the rally it was obvious that Erik was pacing himself, and was determined to finish the event. By the halfway stage he had not opened the enormous lead that had been expected of him, but was lying third, two minutes behind the leading car. However, he had the inbuilt disadvantage of having a high number and losing a lot of time behind the cars in front that got stuck. By inspired driving he managed to regain much of this lost time, but still had to be content with second place, behind a Ford Cortina. Once during the rally, he became stuck in a mud pool, and his car had to be rolled over four times to get it back on to firm ground. The only ill effects suffered by the car were a few dents on the doors and roof. At the finishing line in Nairobi nobody believed this, so the car was turned on to its roof outside Nairobi City Hall, put back on to its wheels and driven away. The winning Cortina was inside the city hall for the prize-giving ceremony, and its crew did not want to be outdone by the Saab. They took their car on to the stage and turned it upside down. Unfortunately they could not turn it on to its wheels again and all the oil and battery acid ran out. The car had to be carried out and it cost $10,000 to repair the hall floor.

After the Safari came the Tulip, which tends to be more of a test of a car's performance than its toughness. The overall placing system is slightly strange and to do well in it a driver has to be very good in his own class and also good compared with the cars in the two adjacent classes. As the Saabs were in the same class as the fast DKW Junior, and had the even faster DKW F12s and 997 cc Cooper Minis in the class above them, they had almost no chance of an overall win. So Pat Moss's sixth overall, Coupe des Dames win and third in class was a very creditable result. The rally was won by a Cooper S Mini. Next came the Acropolis Rally in Greece, an excellent competitive rally with twelve special stages and generally very fast and rough going other than that: in fact only 19 cars finished from almost 70 starters. Pat Moss, in a Group 2 Saab, drove superbly throughout the rally and finished third in the overall classification, winning the Coupe des Dames. She had a completely uneventful rally except for the fact that her windscreen-wiper motor failed in heavy rain and her unlucky co-driver had to operate the wipers by hand under the dashboard whilst crouching on the floor. Erik was also having a very good rally, being well up with the leading cars, and when Paddy Hopkirk retired with his Cooper S he seemed to have a good chance of taking the lead from Tom Trana's Volvo. Unfortunately, Erik went off on one of the last stages and lost over fifty minutes of penalty and so thousands of marks.

The Rally to the Midnight Sun again had more than its fair share of Saabs entered. However, the Group 1 Saabs were at a significant disadvantage in certain of the tests, mainly the tarmac races, as they had to do the same times as the faster Group 1 Volvos and Ford Falcons. This, coupled with the easy category the Group 2 Volvos were racing in, and Tom Trana's brilliant driving, made it unlikely that the Saabs would gain high overall placings. Pat Moss was driving a car with a very tired engine, and Erik had to retire after he put his Saab on to its side at the last bend of the Tierp airfield test. Saab did have the compensation of getting sixth, eighth and ninth in the overall classification, so winning the team award. Next came the Alpine, a hard rally over the French Alps, and very testing for the cars. The biggest disappointment for Saab was Pat Moss's retirement on the very fast Mont Ventous test with a blown cylinder-head gasket, a pity as she had been doing well and might have won the Coupe des Dames. Erik had a good rally, coming second in the touring catagory to a Cortina GT, and winning a Coupe des Alpes, remaining unpenalised on the road section of the rally.

The Polish Rally proved to be very unlucky for the Saab team. They led from the start of the rally, with Erik in first place and Pat in second. However, on the last day one of the Saab service cars fell into a river and could not be extricated to get to a service point and supply the Saabs with fuel, with the result that they both ran out. After about fifteen minutes searching they managed to find a marshal with a jerry can of petrol, which they shared, and continued the rally. Sadly, the lost time could not be made up and they had to be content with second and third placings. On that rally Pat Moss ran out of petrol for a second time and had to fill the tank up with five litres of pure alcohol, carried for de-icing the carburettor. Not surprisingly, even with generous measures of oil added, the car went like a bomb although it kept half seizing and blowing itself free. At the end of the stage she told the mechanics what she had done and they made suitable discouraging noises. However, the car not only finished the rally but was driven back to Sweden with no sign of any ill effects.

The Rally of the 1,000 Lakes provided the remarkable Simo Lampinen with his second international win. At twenty he had already been rallying Saabs for three years and won the Finnish Rally Championship. This was especially impressive because at thirteen he had contracted polio and spent two years in an iron lung. The polio had also left his left foot deformed. This was his first year of international rallying and he had already done well on the Midnight Sun, finishing eighth overall, but had retired from the Acropolis without any brakes left. Saabs also finished third and seventh, thus proving to the rally world that they were still a force to be reckoned with. The Liège, probably the toughest of all the rallies, served to confirm the continued performance of Saab. The 1964 event was in fact the last one ever staged, and was generally considered to be an event more suited to large powerful cars than the small Saabs. It must be noted that the Saabs were Group 4, the engines were tuned to give about 90 bhp and the doors, wings, bonnet and bootlid were plastic. Even so, their performance was remarkable: they were driven almost flat out all the way with good use being made of Erik's co-driver's ability to find the most remarkable short cuts. The works entered only two cars in the rally and Erik took one of them into second overall position, being beaten by a Healey 3000, but beating Bohringer, in the very fast Mercedes 230SL, into third position. Pat Moss took her Saab into fourth place. Interestingly enough no car as small as the Saab had ever even been placed in the Liège before.

The German Rally, always something of an unknown quantity, had to be cancelled. This meant that there was nothing between the Liège and the Geneva. The result of this was particularly significant to Erik as he needed points to consolidate his lead over Tom Trana in the drivers' championship, especially as points he gained in the Alpine were not allowed to count as the organisers felt that there were not enough cars competing in his category. In fact, the Geneva was most suitable for Erik Carlsson and Saab as many of the stages were liberally coated with snow and ice, and he gained a very creditable third overall, while Tom Trana could manage only sixth. Pat Moss came seventh overall, and won the Coupe des Dames.

Erik went into the RAC, the last rally of the season, with an increased lead over Tom Trana, but a piece of bad luck robbed him of the title: on one of the stages there was a badly placed arrow which caused considerable confusion to many competitors, and some to take the wrong turning. Erik took the wrong turning. This took him from a possible winning position to well down the results. It was argued that this stage should have been scrubbed, but the RAC refused, and so Tom Trana won both the rally and the championship. Pat Moss won her class, the ladies prize and was fourth overall in the rally. Pat had already clinched the Ladies Championship for that year, and it was a pity that Erik could not have won the Men's Championship, which he so richly deserved.

The 1964 season was one of mixed fortunes for Saab. It made it obvious that the Saab was outclassed by the 1275 cc Cooper S Mini in terms of speed, although the Mini was not nearly as durable as the Saab and so not at all suitable for rallies such as the Safari. The Ford Falcon and Mustang threat had not materialised to any great extent, and did not look as if it would present anything of a problem in subsequent seasons. Ford of Great Britain were beginning to make their presence felt in quite a big way with the Cortina GT, and looked to be set for quite a rosy future when their reliability problems had been solved. The Volvo P544 and the Healey 3000, hardly new to the rallying scene, were both still very competitive. Without doubt there was nothing to touch the Saab in its own capacity class, and on loose roads it was also almost unbeatable, but it simply did not have the power to be the all-conquering car that it was in 1962 and 1963. A new version with more power was badly needed if Saab were to continue with a competitive rally car.

Saab and Colour

Saab's policy with regard to colour is interesting. The single-colour policy had ended in December 1952 with the introduction of the 92B. Six different colours had then been introduced, which set the seal to a policy of having a fairly modest range of colours, yet with an acceptable amount of variety. The 1953 colours were light grey, blue grey, black, light green, tan and maroon. Not, perhaps, the most inspiring selection of colours but a reasonable selection for the period—and at least you had a change from green. In late 1953 synthetic paints replaced the cellulose. Saab's policy has generally been to change one or two colours each year, thus enabling them to drop unpopular colours and give a certain distinctiveness to each year's model, whilst still retaining their basic modest range. Here is an example: by 1962 their range had become pearl grey, black, light blue, grey, white and red. In 1963 green and dark blue replaced pearl grey and black. In 1964 glacier blue and savannah brown replaced green and light blue and in 1965 olive replaced grey. The tendency towards richer hues (away from black and innumerable shades of grey) was continued in later years. This was partly because bright colours for cars were getting more popular, and partly that an increasingly safety-conscious age considered that grey toned too well with tarmac to be comfortable. More oranges and yellows were appearing in the colour charts—blues and greens were becoming brighter. The staple bright colour for Saab had always been red, for the simple reason that red was the colour of most rally cars for many years and so the colour that most people associate Saab with. It is probably true to say that red is the colour to have had the longest run in the Saab colour charts. Saab, like the rest of the motor industry, suddenly discovered that, with the addition of some superbly irrelevant epithet, quite ordinary colours were transformed into far more exciting ones. Red became 'toreador red' and 'cinnabar red'; medium blue became 'Caroliner blue', green became 'Tyrol green', 'Emerald green' and 'Verona green'—even white could not escape and became 'Polar white'. Indeed, what potential Saab owner could resist the glamorous appeal of 'Silversand' or 'Silvermink' (or, indeed, 'Acacia green metallic'). In 1959 a new paintshop was built at Trollhattan, obviously with the introduction of the 96 in mind. The new shop was large and bright, and so designed that the atmosphere could be kept free of dust and fumes with only the use of underfloor water absorption. This shop was used for painting all model 95 body shells brought up from Linkoping for painting and taken back again for assembly. The body shells were first vacuum cleaned and inspected, then sent on a long overhead conveyer over the factory car park to the phosphating bay. They were degreased, then phosphatised by the zinc phosphate method. After drying and filling the body was passed through a 65 ft long drying oven at a temperature of 347°F. All the body joints were then closed with a rubber based sealing compound. The body was spirit washed and tack ragged, then primed and baked again. At this stage the under-body was hot sprayed with underseal. It was then prepared for the finishing coat, of which it received two double coats, stoved for 30 minutes at 302°F. The paint was brought up in pressurised tanks rather than by pipeline, and the policy tended to be that a separate colour would be used for each day's production. This advanced system established the principles followed today.

A New Nose

In September 1964, just over nine years after its introduction, the characteristic 'nose' of the Saab was altered to make it almost unrecognisable. The overall length of the car was increased by about 7 in—this was entirely on the front overhang. The front wings obviously had to be extended, and in this redesigning they lost the gentle radius of the old wings and gained an angle of almost 90°, thus facilitating the fitting of a front panel that was essentially flat and vertical. The bonnet became flatter and the raised central section far less pronounced. The car had gained a full-width radiator grille, rather unusual as the grille was a series of perforations in the panel itself rather than a hole covered by some bright metal structure. The headlamps were mounted at each top corner of the panel, within the pierced-metal section. The shape of the older Saab grille had been retained in a somewhat altered form: a bright-metal frame was mounted in the centre of the panel. It was as if the old grille had been inverted and considerably narrowed. The top section of this frame was mounted on the front of the bonnet, and the bottom of the frame extended below the general area of perforations. This quite effectively broke up what would otherwise have been rather a plain front. Two bright-metal strips tapered slightly from the central frame to the headlamps. The Saab logo was retained in the middle of the central frame—it was rather bigger, in fact—but the aeroplane motif was dropped from the front. The bottom of the central frame was flanked by four slits. The sidelight/flasher units were moved from their old positions on the front wings to the bottom corners of the front panel. The front valance had become more an integral part of the car, following the sweep of the wings and front panel. In turn the plates between the bumper and the body became largely unnecessary and were deleted. The bumpers were completely new. The heavy, deep bumpers gave way to much slimmer and shallower ones, tapering down to a very narrow vertical face. The overriders were slightly changed in keeping with the bumpers. The new bumpers were fitted to the front and back of all the saloons, but only to the front of the estates as the old bumper was too much of an integral part to be changed easily at the rear.

The bonnet no longer hinged from the overriders as the front had become stress-bearing after the lengthening of the nose. In fact, the bonnet itself became part of the structure of the car when closed. It was released from the inside of the car by pulling a control under the dash at the left of the car—a T-handled pull of the type used for the freewheel. This raised the front of the bonnet, which then had to be further released with a catch. The bonnet could then be pulled forward a little way on its runners and tilted forward. This most unusual method meant that weight and cost on additional

61

strengthening could be saved as the bonnet was being used to the full, forming a rigid box of the nose of the car. Under-bonnet space was obviously significantly extended. This extra space was partly used for the redesigning of the engine cooling system along more modern lines, with the engine behind the radiator rather than in front of it. With the radiator at the front of the car it was no longer necessary to have the bulkhead behind the engine—the loss of strength from its removal was partly compensated for by the intrinsic strength of the closed engine compartment and partly by the addition of a tie bar across the engine compartment just ahead of the spring mountings. The removal of the radiator also made the round holes in the wheel arches, that had served as air-extraction points, redundant. They were therefore deleted. However, all 95s and 96s bear a reminder of them in the form of two circles pressed into the wheel arches behind the spring mountings. The loss of the vast opening bonnet of the 'round nose' was unfortunate in terms of ease of repair to the engine. However the new bonnet was certainly larger than average, and for more major repairs the front panel was easily removable. In addition to this, the front wings, never hard to remove, were made even easier by the fact that the self-tapping screws had been moved around 90° and so screwed down from the top of the wings.

The heating and ventilation system had been redesigned, and some of the extra room under the bonnet had been utilised to replace the old cardboard heater box with a more modern pressed steel one of a different shape.

The clutch was altered to hydraulic operation. This meant that the clutch became smoother in action. It also meant an end of the old cable that had a nasty habit of removing itself from its channel. The pedals became suspended, which supposedly resulted in an easier action. This raised the two hydraulic cylinders off the floorpan of the car, and necessitated their mounting quite well up on the bulkhead between the engine and passenger compartments. This meant that the separate hydraulic fluid reservoir, which had been mounted on the bulkhead next to the radiator, could be deleted and the cylinders themselves could incorporate reservoirs and also that, on the right-hand-drive versions the battery was moved to the left of the car, whilst on the left-hand-drive it remained on the right. The engine was modified to marginally increase its output. The new engine can be differentiated visually by the modifications done to the cylinder head. Obviously with the fan at the front of the engine, no drive shaft from the fan belt was needed and the mounting for the fan could be cast into the front of the cylinder head. The modification increased the standard engine from 38 to 40 bhp, and the Sport engine from 52 to 55 bhp. The outer drive joints were changed.

It is largely a matter of personal taste as to whether the new front improved the styling of the car or not. In terms of the 96, the area in front of the windscreen represented a high percentage of the car's overall length. It might be said that the 'round nose' 96 was in balance in terms of length of nose to length of body, and that the uncompromising roundness of the old nose complemented the styling of the rest of the car almost perfectly. Certainly the new nose was in a far more modern idiom than the old, but its clean-cut, almost hard-edged, styling was hardly in keeping with a body which did not even have a hint of a hard edge. Without doubt, Saab were faced with a problem. They had a car with styling that was out of step with the rest of the motor industry (with the possible exception of Volkswagen), yet they did not have the money or the inclination to totally redesign it—1964 was the year that the design of project 'Gutmund' was finalised. All the same, for reasons which became clear a little later, they needed to change the image of the car somewhat, and have more room under the bonnet. The new front provided Saab with a workable compromise, so it is perhaps unfair to criticise them too much when their criterion was economic reality rather than aesthetic perfection. In terms of the 95 it might be said that the new nose was a distinct improvement. The 'round nose' 95 had always looked slightly strange—the longer estate body with its use of hard edges had never really suited the short, round nose. With the new nose the 95 gained a new balance.

The 1965 Rally Season

The 1965 Monte Carlo was, like the 1963 event, hit by snow. This removed the speed advantage of the bigger cars and enabled the superior slippery-condition handling of the Saab to be used to greater effect. This being the case, the Saab's power deficit was less of a handicap. The Saabs also benefited from starting in Stockholm because the bulk of the snow was encountered by the competitors who started from Athens and Monte Carlo, as in 1963. From the Swedish start, the Saabs had to travel through East Germany, Poland and Czechoslovakia to reach France. This run was fairly easy as very little snow was encountered up to Gerardmer. From this point on, it began to snow heavily and got progressively worse. It was so cold that the quartz iodine lamps on the Saab, which burn at a very high temperature, kept icing over to such an extent that the car had to stop regularly while the ice was chipped off them. Most of the cars that were dropping out did so not because of any mechanical failure but because conditions were so bad that it was impossible to make some of the controls without losing over an hour, and this meant automatic disqualification. Erik Carlsson came very close to falling foul of this rule on the Col de Granier. He had passed a large number of cars and the snow had been whipped up under the bonnet of the Saab, and completely blocked off the carburettors. He and his co-driver, Gunmar Palm, removed most of the snow but the carburettors were still very much iced up and it took them 57 minutes to get the car going again. It is an indication of Erik Carlsson's brilliant ability that he drove the remainder of the rally without losing any time. And so, being inside the 60-minute time clause, was classed as a finisher. At the end of the rally, before the mountain test, Erik was lying thirty-fourth overall. After this stage, he had raised his overall position to fifteenth, by completing the test without losing time, a remarkable achievement equalled only by Bohringer. Pat Moss drove impeccably throughout the rally, an excellent third overall, the highest ever ladies placing in a Monte, winning her class and the Coupe des Dames. Saab won the team prize with their three works cars (the third driven by Ove Andersson), and three privately entered cars were in the first 35 finishers. Certainly a disappointing rally in that Erik Carlsson would probably have finished in the first three had it not been for the unfortunate incident with the snow. However, overall the result was a good one for Saab as in a very tough rally all their works cars finished, beating a lot of more modern cars which were, on paper, faster.

This was the first year that the Swedish was run as a winter rally, and Saab should really have cleaned up in all the snow and ice. However they had rather bad luck. Ake Andersson drove well— rather like a 1950s Erik Carlsson—and came first in his class and second overall. Ove Andersson received a class second. The real Erik Carlsson was progressing in his usual way when he slid into a ditch on the first stage. Although he was extricated and set up some fast times on the subsequent stages it was not possible to cancel out the 2,000 point penalty. Simo Lampinen was also doing well until a piece of dirt lodged in his carburettor jet on a special stage and reduced his speed to a walking pace. Pat Moss and Liz Nystrom naturally, although not easily, beat the Volvos to win the ladies prize.

The East Africa Safari was, to say the least, eventful. Erik and Pat were in works cars, and there were quite a number of privately entered cars (some of which were not allowed to take part because they were the 'long nose' type which had not been homologated). Erik had Stirling Moss as his co-driver, but unfortunately they got lost. The reason given for this was that excessive wheelspin had ruined the calibration on their Speedpilot so they did not know how far they had come. It was all somewhat academic as they were forced to retire with water in the petrol. Pat, driving with Liz Nystrom, drove superbly but had rather bad luck. The springs on her car were poor from the beginning, although this hardly explains how she came to hit a cliff and lose most of her lights. Worse was to come when her back axle came adrift, acquiring lateral as well as vertical movement. As there did not seem to be much that they could do about it at the time they drove on for over 30 miles at about 60 mph until they reached a rather bemused service crew. The car was jacked up and the wheels fell off. The car had a winch and cables in case it had to be hauled out of mud. So the mechanics fixed one end of the cable to the bottom of the boot, ran it round the back bumper, round the back axle and back into the boot. The cable was then attached to the winch so that it could be tightened up if the cables stretched. As they did not have time to replace the shock absorbers they continued without them (with Erik and a mechanic following them). At one control the cars were inspected to see that there had been no change of shock absorbers—the officials were amazed to see the car running without shock absorbers, but could not give them any penalty points. The shock absorbers were quickly replaced after that. Soon after this there was an unfortunate incident which involved driving into a lorry and damaging the front suspension to such an extent that the steering rack came loose. The hard-working mechanics took the end of the cable that was wrapped around the back axle, fed it through the bulkhead into the engine compartment, round the steering rack and back on to the winch again so that the back axle and steering rack were interconnected and could be tightened up on the same winch. The girls managed to finish the rally, but were disqualified because they had lost too much time on the second leg—they had been leading at the end of the first leg. A disappointment, but quite an achievement to finish.

No works cars were entered in the Tulip, but B. Lund and Olle Dahl came first and second in the touring category in privately entered cars. A team was entered in the Acropolis. Erik came second, a few seconds behind Carl Magnus Skogh in a Volvo, after a battle which had lasted the whole rally. Ake Andersson finished fourth, but Pat Moss had to drop out with gearbox failure. In the Gulf London Rally Pat came fifth and Jerry Larsson came second (Ford Cortina GTs took nine of the first twelve places). In the Polish, Saab took the team prize with Erik coming third, Pat fifth, and winning the ladies prize, and Ove Andersson coming sixth.

Simo Lampinen did not win the 1,000 Lakes Rally as he had done in the previous two years, but only because his Saab was under-powered compared with the Cooper Ss. He gained a creditable fourth place. The Tour de Corse was rather unlucky for one pri-vately entered Saab: the drivers had been told that it was not a rough rally, and so they did not bother to bring a skidpan. Not surprisingly they retired very early in the rally without an exhaust system. Saab had very bad luck on the RAC, having extensive engine trouble on all the cars except Pat's. Ove Andersson retired early with crankshaft failure, Ake Andersson and Hans Lund with piston failure and Erik was greatly slowed down by it. However, he and Jerry Larsson fought hard, pushing Makinen and Aaltonen right to the end and coming fourth and third respectively. Pat came tenth overall, first in the ladies class and second to Erik in Class 9. This meant also that she became European Champion.

The Search for a New Engine

In the early 1960s serious consideration was being given to a replace-ment for the three-cylinder, two-stroke engine in the 95/96 body. It is interesting to note that at the same time the type of engine to be used in 'Gudmund' was also being considered, though it may be said that there was almost no connection between the two projects. The three-cylinder, two-stroke engine was thought to have rather a limited life by some people, because, as the standard of small four-stroke engines was improving, the two-stroke was finding it difficult to compete on performance and fuel economy. There was also a certain amount of resistance in certain markets to two strokes with the inconvenience of adding the oil to the petrol and the characteristic, though much reduced, trail of blue smoke. There were two schools of thought within Saab: first that there was a future in a new two-stroke engine, and second that, whilst there was a short-term future with two strokes, the long-term future had to be with four strokes. The less-than-wonderful sales figures in these years seemed to bear out the latter contention. In 1962 it was decided to move along three different paths in engine development. First, and least controversially, further development of the three-cylinder engine. Second, testing to destruction a number of small foreign four-stroke engines. Third, the development of a two-stroke engine along rather different lines from the three-cylinder unit.

As regards the last project, work was being done on a V4 two-stroke engine. This configuration was chosen because it seemed ideal in external dimensions for the 95/96. Prototypes of this engine were produced in two configurations, first with the carburettor in the centre of the V and the exhaust outside. Second with the carburettors outside the V and the exhaust in the centre. The first prototype was soon rejected as it made pulse-charging almost impossible. The second prototype could be designed to have a pressure wave, but the technical problems in producing a reliable engine were insurmountable. It proved to be very difficult to take care of the heat in the centre of the engine from the exhaust manifold. Carburation was also a problem: one carburettor for each bank was needed as it proved impossible to obtain good gas flow with one centrally placed carburettor. When fitted to the outside of the banks the carburettors proved to be too far from the centre of the engine, and so troubled by vibration. In addition this arrangement made the engine too wide. Probably the most important reason for the engine's rejection was that its performance was disappointing. Even with a properly tuned exhaust system, the specific power was less than the three-cylinder unit. The pressure sequence could never be ideal on a four-cylinder engine, the pressure curve falling sharply from its peak. So it would not be possible to obtain a flat torque curve. It was decided that the project had no practical future, and it was abandoned.

Meanwhile the three-cylinder, two-stroke engine was being further refined. The main problem that remained that could be improved on was that of distribution of wet fuel. It was discovered, with the help of a plexiglass window fitted to the inlet manifold, that at very low speeds the centre cylinder received the greatest part of the fuel. However, as soon as the engine speed got above 200 rpm, as soon as the engine started, the greater part of the fuel followed the sides of the induction manifold and so the outer cylinders received it, the centre cylinder being relatively starved. At first there were attempts to develop a better system whilst retaining the single carburettor. Much work was done in the way of introducing baffles into the inlet manifold in order to direct the wet fuel to cylinder two, with only limited success. Work was done in co-operation with Ricardo in developing a drum-shaped mixing chamber to go under the carburettor in which the fuel and air mixture was rotated before going into separate channels. This effectively solved the distribution problem but produced very little power. Reed valves were studied as a possible way of reducing pressure variations within the induction system, and they were shown to provide satisfactory levels of performance, but were not sufficiently reliable. Sleeve valves were discarded as being too expensive and complex, so not worthwhile designing into the engine. The only reasonable alternative remaining for Saab was to design a triple-carburettor system. This was not new as it had been used with some success on a number of competition engines. It effectively solved the problem of uneven fuel distribution as each cylinder would get an even amount of fuel if the carburettors were adjusted properly. In addition, it actually improved performance. The three-carburettor system provided improved torque and bhp figures throughout the range. Particularly noticeable was the important low-speed torque figure. So it seemed to provide the solution to the problem of induction.

At the same time the engine was modified to be fitted into the new 'long nose' body. The standard engine had its output increased to 40 bhp at 4,250 rpm, and its torque to 60 lb ft at 3,000 rpm. The compression ratio was increased to a normal 8·1:1, and the crankcase compression to 1:1·39. The timing was altered somewhat and the carburettor was new: not the triple-carburettor set-up, but a single Solex BI. As the radiator had been moved to the front of the engine, the fan took its drive from the water pump, which had been cast into the front of the cylinder head, as had the thermostat. This provided a significant improvement in cooling, along with the larger air intake of the new front. This improved cooling was needed for the standard engine, but especially for the new Sport engine. This produced 55 bhp at 5,000 rpm, and torque at 66·5 lb ft at 4,000 rpm. The compression ratio had been raised to a nominal 9·1:1, and the crank-case compression to 1:1·46. The timing was changed and the ports were generally cleaned up and polished. The exhaust system was also somewhat modified, and the carburettors were the triple Solex 34W. To begin with they had problems with a rich mixture at low revs, solved by making the air in the air cleaner pass through three small tubes—one to each carburettor. This, on the principle of the Helmholtz resonator, effectively increased the velocity of the in-coming air at low speeds. Some of these engines also got rather a bad name for poor petrol consumption. This is not entirely fair. The problem centred around the adoption of separate adjustment controls on each of the three carburettors. This made them difficult to adjust, and accurate adjustment of the slow-running was very important. Many of the early cars were not adjusted properly and were uneconomical. Later cars were fitted with a common throttle and adjustment screws and so were much easier to keep in tune. Of course it was not an economical car when all the extra available power was used, anyway. It is interesting to note that the SU electric petrol pump was abandoned on both engines in favour of a mechan-ical one. With the Sport engine some early problems were experienced with runaway pre-ignition causing seized and burnt pistons. After considerable tests it was discovered that the best way to cure this was to use a cold-type sparking plug with an auxiliary gap to prevent early discharge from the electrodes.

The extra power developed by the Sport engine caused the question of lubrication to be raised. There were some doubts as to whether petroil lubrication would be efficient enough to deal with the extra strain imposed on the engine. The problem could have been overcome by increasing the percentage of oil in the petrol, but this would not have been ideal as it would have increased the cost to the customer, and made the unpopular two-stroke smokiness more obvious. It was therefore decided to adopt some form of separate lubrication system. The DKW system of feeding oil from an under-bonnet reservoir directly into the carburettor was obviously examined, but rejected on the grounds that it hardly constituted any advance upon the existing system. Saab engineers became convinced that the best system would be a separate lubrication pump feeding the main bearings and the cylinder bores. Therefore a system was designed with an oil tank to the right-hand side of the engine with a pump near the front of the block driven from the crankshaft. This would pressure-feed oil to each of the four main bearings, and to the wall of each cylinder at points near the inlet ports. Naturally the system was very expensive for Saab to instal as it entailed modifying the castings for the cylinder block and the lower half of the crankcase so that oil channels could be cast in. However it proved to be a good system with a very low incidence of failure, and the oil consumption of the engine was significantly lower than that of petroil engines. With this engine Saab had probably the best two-stroke engine of its day, and certainly the best they ever produced. The life of the standard engine was further prolonged by fitment with the triple-carburettor system, though not separate lubrication.

In August 1965 the 1966 models were introduced. The standard engine was again modified, this time to give 42 bhp. This was achieved by replacing the single carburettor with three small carburettors on a new manifold. This significantly improved the efficiency of the engine as no cylinder would be starved of mixture. The modification also made the car much smoother and radically altered the note of the engine. It lost much of its two-stroke 'put-put', and gained an almost jet-like whine. The carburettor change and a cut in the percentage of oil added to the fuel, cut down the visible exhaust significantly. The three-speed gearbox was finally deleted, all Saabs coming with the all synchromesh four-speed gearbox as standard. The new outerdrive joints of the previous year were joined by new constant-velocity inner drive joints. The hubcaps and rear lights were slightly modified, and all 95s and 96s on the Swedish market came with two exterior mirrors as standard equipment. The Saab Sport, for 1966 the Monte Carlo 850 on all markets, gained a new final drive and an alternator. In America and Switzerland a new model was introduced, called the Special, available in either 95 or 96 form. It consisted of a car in standard trim but with a Monte Carlo engine, disc front brakes and a tachometer. This meant that the Saab owner did not need to make do with a 2+2 if he wanted the extra performance. Of course this was largely an interim measure, as Saab needed to retain their credibility in important markets until the introduction of the V4.

The 1966 Rally Season

The fact that Saab were not allowed to compete in the Monte Carlo Rally because the cars could not be homologated in time must have been disappointing, especially as it was not their fault. In the event the 1966 rally was no great loss as nobody gained much credit from it. The Swedish Rally provided a very good result. Erik started well and led on the first stage. Simo Lampinen had redesigned the Saab's front suspension and lost seven minutes when he hit a rock, but at the halfway stage Saabs were second, third and fourth. In the second half of the rally Ake Andersson soon took the lead. Erik blew up his car's engine, and this lost Saab an almost certain team prize. Simo Lampinen got into second place behind Ake, and there the two of them stayed. Ake was nearly forced to drop out of the rally with a split gearbox casing, finishing the rally at little more than a crawl, having his gearbox filled every ten kilometres. Saabs also came sixth and seventh, with Pat winning the ladies prize.

There was no official team in the Italian Rally of the Flowers that year, slightly ironic as the handicapping system was such that the Saabs would have had a good chance of winning it. Pat and Erik were taken up with preparations for the East Africa Safari. This was eventful as usual, but perhaps not quite as colourful as in previous years. Pat retired at Dar-es-Salaam when in second place with a badly damaged back axle. Erik moved into second place and became the only European driver left in the event. He was forced to retire halfway round the Mombasa leg with a broken crankcase. He had the misfortune to hurt his back in the Safari and that caused him to be a non-starter in the Acropolis. Indeed the Acropolis was rather an anti-climax for Saab overall. Ollsson retired early, and Pat was forced to retire with a broken crankshaft. In the end Carl Orrenius came fifth overall, winning his class,.and Lund came eighth. After the success of the previous year the Gulf London Rally was flooded with Saabs, and they dominated the rally. Ake Andersson won it, with Pat coming second. She also won her class, the ladies award and the member award.

Erik made his first appearance after his back injury in the Czechoslovakian Rally Vltava. His appearance was rather short-lived as he retired with a petrol union on a carburettor having worked loose, and air being sucked into the carburettors. Pat brought her car into fifth place. This was an old round-nose car, much to everyone's amazement. It seemed that the competition department had a number of old bodies it wanted to use up. The German rally had a very strange ending. A local driver called Raschig came sixth overall in a Saab, but was disqualified when the police brought a prosecution against him for driving offences committed whilst competing. The Alpine was quite an occasion for Saab, the competition debut of the Sonett. However, the occasion fell rather flat when Erik crashed his and had to retire, and Pat retired with mechanical problems. Pat gained the ladies prize in the Three Cities Rally, which counted towards the drivers' championship.

Four works cars were entered in the RAC, all Monte Carlo 850s. They were driven by Erik, Pat, Carl Orrenius and Ake Andersson. Saab were very conscious that their cars were outpaced and it was obvious that the drivers had been told to use higher revs. Ake burnt out a piston and retired. And Carl broke the contact breakers whilst in second place and dropped to eleventh overall. Pat had a relatively uneventful drive and came ninth overall, winning the ladies prize. This rally to all intents and purposes represented the final fling of the works two strokes.

Saab were first overall in the Norwegian Winter Rally and the Swedish Championship.

4 The V4

In the normal course of events all motor manufacturers examine the products of their competitors, often testing them to destruction or stripping them down to the last nut. Saab were, of course, no exception but the testing of small foreign four-stroke engines in the early 1960s was more a concerted programme of testing to try to find a viable alternative to the two-stroke engine for the 95/96, although at the time not everyone within Saab was willing to admit this. A number of seemingly suitable engines were taken and extensively tested. These included the small Lancia V4, the flat 4 Hansa 'boxer' engine, the VW, the Volvo PV444, the Triumph Spitfire and the new Ford V4 'Cardinal' engine. Saab had decided that however much they wanted to design and build the engine themselves they would have to face the fact that because of lack of experience with four strokes and lack of space they would have to buy in an engine. Initially the engines were given a very intensive testing cycle like that used to test the two-stroke engines. They did not perform as well as the two strokes in terms of durability: no engine would run for more than 20 or 30 hours without some adjustment being carried out to the exhaust valves.

In the longer term they were tested to destruction, and the results of this closely studied with two aims in mind. First was to reject engines which would obviously not be suitable—the Spitfire engine was an early casualty, not really of suitable configuration and rather unreliable. The Lancia engine, which at first glance looked right in terms of size and configuration, went the same way. Indeed all the engines were seen to have problems—though obviously some more than others. Of all those examined it is probably true to say that the one looked hardest at was the Ford. It seemed to fit the requirements as far as external dimensions were concerned, and it showed itself passably well on the bench testing, with a great deal of potential for development, the engine being rather new and 'raw'. It may be true to say that the engine was something of an embarrassment for Ford, because after the American 'Cardinal' project was abandoned they had only a limited use for it, and so would have been glad to receive overtures from another company about buying the engine. Certainly Saab and Ford already had something of a special relationship with regard to the engine, as Ford had purchased thirty Saab 96s and fitted the engine to them in order to test it on the roads without attracting attention before the 'Cardinal' project was dropped. Saab were obviously most interested in the results of these tests. The engine was extensively tested by Saab in the cars and it was finally decided at a very high level that this was the engine they wanted. With this in mind high-level negotiations were carried on with Ford in the utmost secrecy about the possible purchase of the engine.

Meanwhile at the factory the project appeared to have been merely a routine engine test to be carried no further. The idea of replacing the two-stroke engine was still highly controversial, and Saab wished everything to go very quietly and without fuss either from within or without. Therefore right until almost the last moment only about half-a-dozen people within Saab knew that the project was serious. An agreement had been reached with Ford to supply a modified version of the engine from Germany fully assembled. The modifications related to such things as strengthening the main bearings, con rods and the like. The engine was to be fitted with a different carburettor and exhaust system and numerous detail changes to adapt it to both the Swedish conditions and the Saab car. With the long-nose body already in production, the car itself needed very few modifications. At the time rumours abounded, but nothing was known for sure, and the secrecy was kept up until the last minute. The launch was to be August 1966, and the changes within the factory to produce the new car were all done very hurriedly in the period of the works shutdown for the summer holiday. Even the brochures for the 1967 model year were allowed to go to press with no mention of anything other than the two-stroke car. Separate brochures were printed at the last minute for the V4. The early V4s came with decals instead of proper badges for similar reasons. So Saab had the best of both worlds—a very fine two stroke for the purists and the practicality of the four stroke for everyone else.

In August 1966 disc front brakes and an alternator became standard on all models. In that same month the V4 was introduced on the Swedish market and to the British market in 96 form in October. The changes that had taken place since the introduction of the long-nose body had effectively prepared the car for the fitting of the bigger engine and very few additions were needed with it. In addition to this a stronger starter motor and a higher capacity battery were also introduced. The interiors were changed in honour of the new engine. The hessian-type cloth inserts were replaced by a complete facing of a closer-weave nylon for the seats, and a buttoned finish was introduced on to the door panels. The door trim and buttoned finish introduced on each side of the rear seat were topped by padded safety strips where before there had just been painted metal. Two large, detachable bins were fitted to the front of the car, under the dash between the leading edge of the door and the wheel arch. It was obvious that the car had been rushed on to the market, and this was effectively illustrated by the V4 badges. At first no badges were ready and simple decals had to be used, then some temporary metal badges became available and were placed high on the front wings. When, eventually, the proper badge was introduced it was rather different in shape and placed low on the front wings behind the wheel arches.

It is interesting to note that Saab seemed interested in emphasising the safety aspect of the V4. One of the introductory adverts read: 'We wondered . . . could we add another safety feature to the Saab? So we did . . . The dynamic acceleration of the new V4 Saab.' This particular advert also suggested that one should: 'GO SWIFT GO SAFE GO SAAB.' *Motor* were impressed by the car, saying it was one of the best cars in its class and represented outstanding value for money. They were slightly puzzled by its rather low gearing, which meant that top speed was obtained at a little over 5,000 rpm rather than 4,750 rpm, the point at which maximum power was reached. This was obviously an inheritance from the two stroke, with its need for ratios to keep the engine speed high. In terms of performance figures *Motor* obtained a mean top speed of 88·3 mph, with a best figure of 91 mph. 0–60 mph time was a very creditable 16·6 sec, and 0–50 achieved in 12·5 sec. The overall petrol-consumption figure obtained was 28·5 mpg without the use of the freewheel. *Motor* suggested that the average owner should have no problem in bettering 30 mpg, and even better than this figure with use of the freewheel. A touring consumption of 35·2 mpg was obtained. Particularly significant was the fact that over 30 mpg could still be obtained at a constant 70 mph. It is interesting to compare the figures with those for the two-stroke Sport. The Sport produced 55 bhp at 5,300 rpm and 67 lb ft torque at 3,800 rpm; the figures for the V4 were 65 bhp at 4,700 rpm and 83 lb ft at 2,500 rpm. The Sport's mean top speed was 85 mph, with a best figure of 90·9, while the 0–60 mph time was 18·9 sec, though 0–50 took 12·3 sec. Acceleration times in third and top were better in the V4, in some cases significantly so. Overall petrol consumption was 21·6 mpg and touring consumption 30·6. At a constant 70 mph consumption was 25. With the V4 selling at £801 and the Monte Carlo selling at £1,058 it is not surprising that very few Monte Carlo 850s were sold after the introduction of the V4.

On the Scandinavian and British markets the V4 96 came with the same trim as the two stroke; on the American market the V4 96 came with the same external trim as the Monte Carlo. The two stroke in America was rather basic—having drum brakes on all wheels, a dynamo rather than an alternator, a smaller battery and starter motor, single-speed windscreen wipers, all-vinyl upholstery and a slimmed tool kit. It came with two engine alternatives: one with petroil and the other with separate lubrication. The 55 bhp Special was no longer available as its place in the market had been taken over by the V4. The 95 V4 was not introduced to the British market until January 1967.

The fact that the V4 had proved to be Saab's salvation is vividly illustrated by examination of Swedish sales figures for 1967 and 1968. In 1967 almost 24,000 V4s were sold, against only 500 two strokes, and in 1968 over 30,000 V4s were sold against only 28 two strokes. The figures from 1964 to 1968 make the picture even clearer: 1964, 29,000 cars sold; 1965, 26,000 cars sold; 1966, 19,000 cars sold (of which 8,000 were V4s); 1967, 24,500 cars sold and 1968, 30,000 cars sold. In Britain the V4 cost only £59 more than the standard two stroke. This was not the most important point in the remarkable sales of V4s and the remarkable lack of sales of two strokes, but it is not without its significance. In early 1967 the Monte Carlo 850 was replaced by the Monte Carlo V4 and except for the engine the two cars were identical. The Monte Carlo 850 was dropped partly because its sales had fallen almost to nothing and partly because factory competition work was carried out largely in V4s which made the two-stroke car something of an anomaly, as well as something of an embarrassment. It was something of a disappointment, however, that the Monte Carlo V4 came with a standard 65 bhp engine rather than something more powerful.

The 1967 Rally Season

Saab did not bother to enter a works team in the 1967 Monte Carlo Rally, so their first rally was the Swedish. This was the first official run of the V4, and it was being driven very carefully. Simo Lampinen came in second and Olle Bromark was seventh. Quite reasonable for a debut, though it would have been nice to have won it. In February Ake Andersson left the Saab team and joined Porsche. Pat entered the V4 in the Italian Rally of the Flowers—unfortunately she was not allowed to start as the cars' papers had been left at Trollhattan, and although Erik promised to have them flown down before the end of the rally the officials remained adamant. Erik and Pat did not enter the East Africa Safari, though a car entered by the Mayers came home with a Class 1 win. In the Tulip Pat had the embarrassment of stripping the car's drive-shaft splines on the starting line of the first test. She did go on to win the ladies prize though.

In the Austrian Alpine there were four Saabs entered: two V4s from the factory driven by Arne Hallgren and Lasse Jonsson, and two privately entered cars driven by Torsten Palm and Stig Blomqvist. Lasse drove very well to come second—he would have been first but he lost three minutes near the end when he got lost. Arne came eighth, and Saab won the National team prize. There was no Saab team for the Acropolis, but a full team was entered in the Czechoslovakian and Erik and Pat came first and second.

In the 1,000 Lakes Simo Lampinen set a very fast time in the early stages, and was in the lead, being pressed hard by Makinen in a Cooper S. The two cars vied for the lead throughout the rally and in the end Makinen just beat Simo into second place. Tom Trana had very bad luck, first part of the fan shot through his radiator, causing the car to overheat and the head gasket to leak. Then the coil lead fell off and the gearbox failed—Tom therefore felt that it might be wise to retire. Saab received the team award, having three cars in the first ten. There was no RAC that year as there was an outbreak of foot and mouth disease and the passing rally cars would have contributed to the spreading of the disease.

Saab came first overall in the Riihimaki Rally, the Norwegian Winter, the Hankiralli and the Norwegian Rally.

Changes for 1968

The 1968 Saab, announced in late 1967, contained a number of valuable improvements. Perhaps the advertisement headline 'A New Saab (You didn't really think that we would rest on our laurels. We have improved the V4 on 21 points)' might have been laying it on a bit thick, though. The most important improvement was the deepening of the windscreen by 7 cm. This, coupled with the enlarged rear window on the 96 model, improved visibility considerably and countered what had been one of the main criticisms of the 96. Both windscreen and rear window were enlarged upwards. With the new windscreen came larger wipers and electric windscreen washers. The instrument panel was painted dark grey to make it more neutral and less reflective and for the same reason the steering wheel was finished in black. The smart black-and-chrome steering-wheel boss with its chrome horn ring was dropped in favour of a larger black plastic padded boss, which was safe, if rather ugly. Still in pursuit of safety the door locks were improved as were the interior door handles. The brake pipes, instead of running down the centre of the floorpan where they would be corroded by any water that settled there, were run down the side along the sills and away from harm's way. The interiors themselves were also improved, as were the seat belts. The two-stroke models retained the lighter grey fascia and rubber mats and all had red and grey upholstery. The actual models made during 1968 were the 95 V4 and 96 V4 on all markets with certain detail changes for individual conditions. The 95 and 96 two stroke was fitted with 46 bhp engines for all markets except America. The American two stroke came in the form of the 'Shrike'. This had the basic trim of the previous year's model and did not have the new body. It also had a detuned engine reduced in capacity to about 800 cc. This brought it to below the 50 cu in limit and thus below the level for the new American emission regulations. The car was available in both 95 and 96 forms, and catered for people who wanted an extremely tough and durable car without paying too much for it. A 95 V4 city delivery van was available on certain markets. The Monte Carlo V4 was dropped and in its place at the top of the range came the 96 V4 De Luxe. This came with the exterior trim of the Monte Carlo, and De Luxe badges (of which there were many). The interior was as for the 96. This was a very smart car and only available on export markets. In America the car came with Monte Carlo instruments, and the Americans also had an estate version, called the 95C.

The 1968 Rally Season

The first rally was the Swedish. Saab entered a works team composed of Tom Trana, Simo Lampinen and Carl Orrenius, and of course there were numerous private Saabs. Carl retired when he hit a fully grown moose on special stage eight—amazingly he managed to finish the stage, but it was too late to repair the car for it to carry on in the rally. Simo retired when the exhaust manifold burnt through his oil-cooler feed pipe. He tried to bypass it, but to no avail. Tom Trana came second, with Hakan Lindberg third, Stig Blomqvist sixth, Jerry Larsson seventh and Per Eklund ninth. Tom Trana and Carl Orrenius were entered in the Monte Carlo but in a dry rally they had little chance of doing very well. Tom Trana finished sixteenth overall. Carl Orrenius blew a cylinder-head gasket and it could not be changed in time for him to continue the rally. There was no official team in the Tulip, but a private entrant kept the flag flying, albeit rather low, with a fourth in class.

The Scottish Rally had a full Saab team entered—Carl Orrenius, Simo Lampinen and Jerry Larsson. The highlight of the rally was the struggle between Carl Orrenius and Roger Clark for the lead. Unfortunately this struggle ended rather abruptly when Carl missed a turning and broke a universal joint while reversing back on to the road. Simo Lampinen came fourth overall. Carl Orrenius had better luck in the Gulf when he came third overall. J. Svensson came eighth. Jerry Larsson was forced to retire with a broken drive shaft.

Simo Lampinen came second in the Rally of the 1,000 Lakes. He would probably have been first but was plagued with clutch trouble. The RAC Rally was very successful for Saab, but also raised many questions. Simo Lampinen was first and Carl Orrenius second, having been second and third at the halfway point. Simo had to have his differential changed at Betws-y-Coed, Tom Trana was forced to retire when his differential locked up solid. Lindberg also had trouble with his differential, and finally retired with engine trouble and problems of overheating.

Saab came first overall in the Hankiralli, the Norwegian Winter Rally, the Norwegian Rally and the Swedish Championship.

5 The 99

In 1969 the 96 was again restyled but, making this a very important year for Saab, the 99 was introduced. The front of the 95 and 96 was redesigned to give it a more modern look and bring it in line with the new 99. The central Saab grille was retained in a slightly changed form—the frame was retained but the plain pierced metal was replaced by twelve chromed horizontal bars. The pierced metal on each side of the central grille was deleted and replaced by nine horizontal chromed bars. The four slits below the grille were also deleted. The European models no longer had round headlamps, but rectangular ones mounted in heavy chrome rims—these lights were said to have improved low beam over the old ones. This may have been true, but more striking was the change in character of the front of the car brought about by the new lamps. It was as if the long-nose body had finally reached maturity—the new front had given it a much deserved air of sophistication. The small indicator/sidelamps on the front panel were deleted and their place was taken by large lamp clusters halfway up the front wings. These consisted of a white section at the front to act as a sidelight, which took up perhaps 25 per cent of the overall length of the lamp. The remainder was amber, and its lens was divided into two distinct facets—one to be seen from the front and the other from the side. This lamp was almost certainly the best on the market at the time and has seldom been bettered since. Other changes included the fitting of rubber inserts to the overriders and redesigned hubcaps, which were more modern in appearance, being less domed and with the central badge altered and accentuated. These hubcaps were in line with those on the 99.

Less immediately obvious changes included alteration of the steering ratio to try to alleviate heavy steering at low speeds. The steering column was made telescopic so that in the event of an accident it would collapse rather than impale the driver. A cross-flow radiator was fitted, as was an expansion tank. This was somewhat more compact than the old radiator. Of the unseen changes, probably the most significant from the point of view of the driver was the addition of a vacuum servo for the brakes. The car's brakes had always been powerful but in the past had encountered some criticism with regard to rather excessive pedal pressures being required. With the freewheel in use there would be no engine braking and powerful brakes that were easy to use were essential. The servo provided these. The badges were new. The one at the front had regained its aircraft and was placed on a blue background, while the one on the extractor vents on the 96 was also blue. The 95 had its rearlamp cluster redesigned to incorporate reversing lights. Because of American legislation the American 95s and 96s looked rather different from the European as they were fitted with round sealed-beam headlights. It might at first glance seem a considerable inconvenience to Saab to have to produce two slightly different frontal designs. In fact the American front became very useful to the company as it was used extensively on rally cars, the theory being that the American front had more grille area than its European counterpart, and so cooled the engine better. This was very important for competition work so the American front was adopted. The cars for the American market also had round exterior mirrors instead of the usual pear-shaped ones.

Of course the new Saab 95 and 96 were interesting, but what really caused a stir was the introduction of the new model—the 99. It is true that everyone already knew of its existence, but a brand new Saab on the market was no common event, and certainly not one to be ignored. With the benefit of hindsight it may be said that the introduction of this car was an extremely significant event in the history of Saab cars in so much as it marked the start of their movement 'up market'. For the first year of production only the basic model was offered—the two-door saloon with the 1709 cc engine and a manual gearbox. The motoring press did not quite know what to make of it. The car represented a positive movement away from previous Saabs, and yet shared many of the attributes of the earlier cars. To start with the styling caused considerable controversy: the car was criticised for being too chunky, and it was said that the rather dated styling was due to the fact that the design had been frozen in 1964. Others suggested that the Saab with its low nose, high tail and general dart shape was something of a timeless design which was successful because of its very efficiency rather than having to rely on any short-term styling fashion.

Development

In the early 1950s Saab engineers were discussing the shape of a completely new model to be introduced some time in the future. Many sketches were produced and a great variety of concepts were considered, as it was difficult to tell exactly in which way the motor industry was moving. Discussion literally ranged from city cars to utilities. Of course the designer was Sixten Sason, and it is very revealing to study some of his 1950s sketches. One in 1954 shows a car with a stubby tail, a comparatively large, high-roofed passenger compartment, and a continuous area of glass right around the front from rear side pillar to rear side pillar. This theme once established was to characterise all of the remainder of the drawings, although some of the drawings did perhaps depart a little from his strict utility approach and show certain influences of current Detroit trends. These may be written off merely as experiments, rather than serious studies. By the late 1950s the idea of the car having a low nose and a high tail had been established, and there was a tendency for the sketches to show a concave shape, especially around the front and the back. A number of models were built up to a 1:10 scale. The differences between these models were not great, and the final design was chosen partly on aesthetic grounds, but mostly as a result of the extensive programme of wind-tunnel testing. The prototype 'Gudmund' was finally chosen. This had a slightly different tail from the other models, being rather more concave from the roof-line and having a smooth convex curve sweeping up from the rear of the rear wheel arch to meet the concave curve at a point which slightly emphasised the fact that the tail was higher than the nose. The front of the car was probably the plainest of all the models— some having fronts which almost came to a point in the middle, and others square-fronted with the totally flat nose protruding, wedgelike at the bottom. When it had been decided that Gudmund was the model they were after, a 1:5 scale model was built for more extensive wind-tunnel tests. These showed that the model had a drag co-efficient of 0·36 and practically negligible lift. These tests helped the designers and engineers to adjust the weight distribution and the centre of gravity for optimum stability, as well as design the air intakes, extraction points and exhaust outlets for maximum drag. A curved windscreen was also designed. Sason worked largely on his own in terms of design, though he did have two designers working for him—Bjorn Envall, later to become head of the Saab design centre, and the English architect Peter Maddock. Both made a contribution to the design of the 99: many of the early drawings were done by them, and Bjorn Envall played a particularly important part in the later development of the 99 when Sason was too ill to work. Around 1960, the project began to take more positive shape. Saab definitely wished to develop a new model to run with the 95/96 rather than replace it. The car was to be a four- or five-seater saloon of about 1300 cc. Obviously the car was to have all the normal Saab virtues of safety and aerodynamic excellence.

Sason's proficiency as an engineer must not be underrated—the designs he produced were sound in terms of structure as well as styling. He had shown this with the 92. The structure of the car had already been decided—the results of all the drawings in the 1950s held good and all that was left was to finalise the details of the styling. This having been achieved, a full-size mock-up of the car was made, incorporating all the work done to date.

At the same time extensive discussion continued relating to the mechanical side of the car. Obviously front-wheel drive was retained —nothing else was ever considered. Gunnar Ljungstrom was inter-ested in using torsion-bar suspension on the car, but the tight schedule of the programme precluded the extensive development that would have been needed for it to be successful. Saab had no particular desire to equip the car with what must have seemed to them to be rather a doubtful system—at this time they simply could not afford for the car not to succeed. The suspension was therefore developed along very similar lines to that of the 95/96—coils all round, independent at the front. In fact the front suspension was very similar to that in the 96, but the rear suspension was altered in order to improve the ride comfort, in line with the car's projected role. The

U-shaped rear axle of the 95/96 had proved to be very successful in terms of handling and roadholding, but questions had been raised about its performance as regards ride comfort of the rear seat. The 99 was aiming at a sector of the market that valued rear-seat comfort more than superb handling, so the car had to be designed accordingly. The rear axle was made straight. This had the added advantage that it was much easier and cheaper to manufacture. The design was extensively tested both on and off the early prototypes. The drive train was also designed early on in the programme. Their aim was compactness, and so the in-line-with-the-engine design of the 95/96 was quickly rejected as wasteful of space. Saab wanted the gearbox to fit underneath the engine, though they did not wish to repeat the BMC mistake of running the gearbox in engine oil. So the idea of a separate gearbox running underneath the sump was evolved.

When it came to engine choice this largely had to fit into what had already been designed, rather than have the car redesigned around it. Gunnar Ljungstrom once said: 'Engine designers have had too much influence on car design for too long.' Saab's position over the engine for the 99 was rather different from their position over the replacement engine for the 95/96. They wished to be involved in the design and development of an engine and be able to dictate its specification. At the time it seemed likely that this would mean going it alone, and they were quite happy to do this. As for actual engine manufacture, things were not quite so simple. They had no suitable factory though this was hardly an insurmountable problem. Serious consideration was never given to the two-stroke engine for the 99— Saab were moving into a market in which the two-stroke would have been even less acceptable. A version of the V4 was also out because, when fitted with the transmission underneath, it would have had an absurdly high bonnet line. The idea of a flat-four engine had a certain appeal in terms of shape, but was never really considered. The Wankel engine was considered, indeed most manufacturers were looking at it at this time, and German consultants came over to Sweden to discuss the project. Engineers at Saab were particularly impressed with its compactness. It was thought that the engine could be made to collapse down the transmission tunnel in the event of a collision. However, Saab had serious doubts about certain aspects of the engine, particularly lubrication and sealing. The idea was soon shelved without a prototype being constructed. Rolf Mellde once said that the decision over the Wankel engine was one of the hardest he ever had to make in his time at Saab. With the benefit of hindsight it may be seen that he certainly made the right decision, as if Saab had used the engine and had the same experience as NSU it probably would have destroyed them. In the end it was decided that the most realistic alternative was a four-stroke, in-line, four-cylinder engine.

With this in mind they contacted the English engine consultant firm Ricardo. The first fruits of this co-operation came in the form of a 1,300 cc overhead cam crossflow engine which produced 55 bhp. This engine was extensively tested, as was the second engine, a non-crossflow 1,500 cc unit producing 68 bhp. Saab were very pleased with the results of these tests and had almost finalised their plans to use an engine of this type with a crossflow cylinder head. Indeed, in the autumn of 1963 twenty test engines were ordered from Ricardo. At around this time Saab got in contact with the Triumph division of British Leyland as both companies had become aware that they were developing very similar engines. It seems likely that the initial advances were made by Ricardo, with whom both companies did business. Any agreement between the two companies could be of direct benefit to them both as Saab would be able to have their engine manufactured for them by Triumph, and Triumph would be getting the Saab–Ricardo engine, which by then was in quite a late stage of development. As early as April 1964 the two companies had decided to co-operate on the project, although the agreement was not finalised until February 1965.

Meanwhile development work was continuing at Saab with the engine fitted into two prototype 99s. The two cars looked rather different from each other as befitted their differing roles. One was fitted with a 1500 cc engine and looked remarkably like the final 99. The most obvious difference being outside doorhandles from the 96, fixed quarter-lights in the front side windows and different interior trim. Large chrome letters across the front of the bonnet proclaimed that it was a 'Daihatsu'. This car was completed in June 1965 and used extensively for rolling-road testing. This was a particularly taxing test as Saab had designed the test rig themselves so that it would be. The car was also road tested, mainly outside Sweden as it was thought that it might be recognised by its Saab trim from the 96. In January 1966 the car was winter-tested in Sweden. It was constantly modified throughout its life—all major new developments being added to it in order to test them. In fact the car was used until November 1967 and it now resides in the Saab museum at Troll-hattan. The majority of work done to change the car related to suspension adjustment, particularly in respect of the back axle, and strengthening the body. In fact the changes were surprisingly minor, a tribute to the excellence of the initial design. Saab also wanted a less 'risky' car to test within Sweden. For this they hit on a very ingenious solution. A floorpan was built up for a 99 and initially fitted with the 1300 cc engine. Instead of the 99-type body being fitted a 96 body was made to fit it. This entailed cutting the body in half longways and welding in a 6 in wide strip. Everything had to be widened, and a surprisingly good job was made of it. At first glance the car, painted mid-grey, was difficult to tell from a normal 96 and this is what the Saab testers wanted as they did not intend that people should be allowed to study it. When looked at longer the car seems disconcertingly squat and wide, so much so that it became christened Paddan or toad. Like the Daihatsu, it ran many miles and was constantly modified. In fact it was built slightly later than the Daihatsu prototype.

The main difference between the attitude of Saab and Triumph towards the engine was that Saab were thinking of an engine below 1500 cc and Triumph were thinking of one above this size (already having a relatively new 1300 cc unit). It is interesting to note that Triumph used the Saab two-stroke engine in the early prototypes of what later became the Triumph 1300. Saab were coming around to the view that a slightly larger engine than the size that they had first anticipated might be better, so the difference in attitude did not become significant. Therefore the final engine size was about 1700 cc. Saab's main contribution to the project at this point was their great experience in bench-testing engines. They were able to test engines to destruction in ways that Triumph had not even thought of and there is no doubt that without the work they did at this stage the engine would have been much inferior to the one actually developed. The other major influence that Triumph had on the project had to do with their long-term plans for the engine. They were thinking not only in terms of a four-cylinder unit which would be flexible in terms of size, but also a V8 which could ulti-mately replace their six-cylinder unit. This entailed keeping the overall width of the engine as low as possible when it was canted over at 45°. Hence the rather strange arrangement of the valve gear, placed at an angle to the cylinders, and the cylinder-head bolts, parallel with the valves. This obviously entailed wedge-shaped combustion chambers which were not ideal. At this stage Saab were not too unhappy about this as they too wanted to keep their options open. So in their final months the prototypes were running around with the 1709 cc engine fitted to them. The only unfortunate aspect of this was that the drive train was still that designed for an engine of 1300 to 1500 cc, and that is why some drive-train problems were experienced on very early models.

In the autumn of 1967 it was decided that it would be in Saab's best interests to release the car to the press. Details of the co-operation on the engine with Triumph had been released at quite an early stage so most people had a good idea that a new Saab was on the way. And if it was made public the final testing would be much easier and rather more effective. This was because the cars could be driven freely on public roads and public reaction to the cars could be gauged before they were released, so making it more likely that any teething troubles would be solved before the cars went on sale to the public. At this time two cars were released for the press to drive, and everyone who drove them had to fill in a comprehensive questionnaire. This did not satisfy Saab, so in 1968 they produced a run of fifty cars and distributed thirty-six of them to a cross section of the motoring public for six months. These people were chosen from all walks of life and were not only Saab owners (some were even Volvo owners). The cars were driven an average of 10,000 miles each and when they were handed back a very comprehensive form had to be filled in relating to all aspects of the car. This testing was invaluable to Saab as it enabled them to change quite a number of small things. For example, quite a few people complained of vibration from the engine, so the engine mountings were changed. The doors were thought to be rather hard to close so were modified accordingly. Similar minor modifications were carried out on the exhaust system, the ignition key and such minor details. The tests confirmed the fact that Saab had a very good car in the 99. It is interesting to note that if the strict numerical order of designation was to be followed this car should have been the 98. However, it became the 99 because Saab thought it had a better ring to it. By the time that the car was made available to the public on 14 August 1968 they had a very full order book. Of course the engine for the 99 was built in the Triumph plant and shipped out to Sweden—but its history shows it was hardly a Triumph engine.

There seems little doubt that within Saab the idea of fitting a V8 engine to a 99 did have a certain appeal. The firm still wanted to move up market and a V8 would easily enable them to do this, as well as solving any problems of lack of performance that they might have had. With this idea in mind, though at this stage it was not seriously pursued, two or three 99s were fitted with Triumph Stag V8 engines—quite a technical feat. These cars were road tested with special reference to handling and cooling; one was winter tested. The mixture seemed to be a fairly successful one, although Saab did have some problems with the bearings. What really killed the project was the fact that in the early 1970s Saab engineers began to suspect that the next decade would be one in which cars with large engines would become very unpopular because of the rising cost of running them, so the project was dropped before the endurance-test stage. Of course other engines were also being bench-tested at the time, though no other engine ever got as far as being road tested. The Rover V8 was tested, for example, but nothing came of it.

Motor said of the car: 'The 99 is not exceptional for speed, nor indeed for a strong sporting character.' They hit the nail on the head, to the dismay of the sporting fraternity. Here was not a car to compete on equal terms with the sports saloons of Europe, nor was it a car to take the rally world by storm again, but here was the basis of a sensible and safe family car of unusual quality (and hopefully the basis for Saab's prosperity for a considerable time to come). The testers were impressed by the intrinsic refinement of the car with an engine that they felt could not be beaten for refinement and flexibility by any other four-cylinder unit. The handling they thought to be excellent in a safe, rather than a sporting manner. All the testers were impressed by the interior, which they considered to be remarkable for its space and for its comfort. Particularly popular were the front seats, with their anatomically contoured shape that was not accompanied by excessive hardness, and their remarkable range of adjustment. Obviously they found the heating system beyond reproach—the winter driver in Sweden would not last long if it were not. The only things that puzzled them slightly were the retention of the freewheel—a device that had never captured the hearts of British testers, and the fact that the ignition key was between the front seats and could only be removed with the car in reverse. *Motor* summed the car up like this: 'The 99 is something of a trendsetter that we much admire.'

In terms of actual performance figures the car seems less than impressive. The maximum speed of under 95 mph was on a par with the V4, and rather inferior to most of its direct competition. Acceleration was equally uninspiring, though it was rather better in top than it was through the gears from a standing start. Overall fuel consumption was good for its class, though obviously not up to the V4. To place too much emphasis on the car's mediocre performance would, however, be extremely misleading as its strength lay not so much in what it did, but how it did it. The prospective 99 owner would not be likely to be very interested in the fact that his car's competitors had top speeds slightly in excess of its own top speed; nor indeed, that they could reach 60 mph from a rest a couple of seconds before him. He probably would be rather more interested to learn that his car could maintain as high cross-country times as the others because of high cruising speed and good handling, leaving him less tired and having used less petrol. He probably would also be interested in the safety and durability of the car, which resulted from its good design and development and was without doubt far superior to all its quicker counterparts, and probably to most other vehicles on the road. If he was not interested in these things then he would be unlikely to be driving a Saab 99 in the first place.

The 1969 Rally Season

Simo entered a privately-backed V4 Sonett in the 1969 Monte Carlo Rally, and although he had problems with a leaking petrol tank he was ninth overall. However, it was alleged that he missed a secret control and was therefore, in true Monte Carlo fashion, disqualified, even though very few people knew much about this control. In the Swedish Rally there was a considerable number of works Group 2 Saabs entered, and an even larger number of private entrants. Stig Blomqvist was given a works car for the first time. The pace of the rally was set by the Saabs and the Porsches, with nobody else having much of a chance. Unfortunately a recurrence of the differential trouble robbed Simo of first place, and he had to be content with second. Lindberg was fifth, Tom Trana seventh and Stig was eighth.

One Saab was entered in the East Africa Safari, driven by Simo Lampinen who was favourite to win at 7–1. Much to everyone's surprise he did not even get as far as the start, as his engine was totally seized and nobody could work out exactly what was the matter with it. Back in Sweden it was stripped down and the problem was found to be a loose big-end bolt. This did not help Simo as there was no replacement car for him to use at the time. There were no Saabs in the Tulip Rally.

In the Rally Vltava there were two works V4s, driven by Simo Lampinen and Lindberg. Simo had a 'sick' engine which was not expected to last, but taking the car relatively easily he managed to make the finish, though he lost 11 minutes with suspension trouble and could only manage to get fourth place. The other works car crashed when a wheel fell off. Luckily nobody was hurt but the car was out of the rally. In the Scottish Rally in August Simo was first, Nilsson fourth and Lindberg tenth, Saab gaining class wins for both two-stroke and V4 cars.

Three works cars were entered in the 1,000 Lakes Rally. Saab were almost certain of the team prize—Simo was second, Makinen fourth and Tom Trana was highly placed until he crashed, and had to retire. Erik entered a 1700 cc V4 in the American BAJA 1,000 race and came third in his class. A privately entered Saab in the TAP Rally came fifth overall.

The RAC provided a good result for Saab, although certain parts of it were tinged with farce. Simo had the bad luck to blow a head gasket on the first stage, and was forced to retire as he had lost over thirty minutes. However the other Saabs were doing well, especially Carl Orrenius and Tom Trana. Lindberg had rather indifferent luck—spending nineteen minutes in a ditch waiting for enough people to come along to lift him on to the road again. Later in the rally he had to have his gearbox changed in Wales. He drove very well and managed to make up most of the lost ground. Stig Blomqvist went off the road twice in the early stages of the rally, the second time knowing that his teammate Per Eklund was close behind him. He therefore went back down the track a little way to try to warn Per, who was so surprised at all this he went off the track too. The two cars were too badly damaged to continue far, and so both had to retire. The final result was that Carl Orrenius was second overall, Lindberg was fifth, Tom Trana seventh and Jonsson tenth.

Saab were first overall in the KAK Rally, the Norwegian Winter Rally, the Hankiralli, the Riihimaki Rally, the Norwegian Gulf Rally and the Norwegian Rally.

Merger

The year was important for the company as a whole as it became Saab–Scania AB. This came about with the merger of Saab with Scania–Vabis, the large Swedish manufacturer of trucks. This merger brought benefits to both companies in addition to the greater security from a larger market base. Saab had more factories, which with a new model was just what they needed. Of course there is also the question of Volkswagen and Porsche: Scania were the sole Swedish importers for these cars and were having considerable success with them. Naturally, though, the philosophy of 'if you can't beat them you might as well take a share of the profits' played no part in the merger at all. A factory was opened in Finland to make Saab cars. This was on the shores of the Baltic at Nystad, and was jointly owned by Saab–Scania and a Finnish company OY Valmet AB. This proved to be the beginning of a very profitable association. The new company of Saab–Scania was divided into four divisions. These are dealt with in greater depth in the final chapter.

Detail Changes

The changes to the 99 for 1970 occurred in autumn 1969 but were minimal: the car was provided with a cigarette lighter and an extra rear ash tray. The inner drive joints were new and the engine mounting improved. The 95 and 96 came in for rather more changes than the 99. It looked as if the updating which had begun on the outside of the car the previous year was being completed on the

inside. The only exterior change was the recessing of the petrol filler
cap so that it would not be knocked off in the event of the car rolling.
The most obvious change inside the car was a completely new
instrument panel. Two large round instruments were substituted for
the one large, and two smaller instruments. The left-hand instrument
was the speedometer. It was similar to that of the previous model,
having white figures on a black ground, but it was slightly simpler
and neater. The right-hand instrument contained the temperature
gauge at the top and the petrol gauge at the bottom. To the right and
left of the gauges were the warning lights for low charge and oil
pressure. There can be no doubt that the layout was a masterpiece of
clarity. The central clock was deleted and replaced by a black
square with a heavy chromed surround on which '95' or '96' were
placed in chrome letters. This was rather unfortunate as it contributed
nothing to the aesthetic appeal of the dash, and certainly contributed
nothing to the driver's awareness of what the car was doing. The
dash itself was covered with a non-shiny black leathercloth. This
effectively made the dash neutral and absorbed reflection, also
giving the whole interior an air of quality in pleasant contrast to the
slightly spartan air of the painted dashes. The old pull switches for
the lights and the heater fan were replaced by two tumbler switches,
which on the right-hand-drive cars were to the right of the instruments, and to the left on left-hand-drive cars. These switches were
easier for the driver to operate, and better positioned. In addition
to this they no longer protruded from the dashboard in a way which
could have been dangerous in an accident. The light switch was
particularly neat—Saab had thought that drivers trying to find the
fan switch at night could accidentally press the light switch and
plunge themselves into darkness. This problem was overcome by
fitting a safety catch to the light switch so that it needed two distinct
movements to switch the lights off. The headlights switched off
with the ignition, so that the battery would not be drained by their
accidentally being left on with the car parked. The glove compartment received a new lock which was rather easier to use than the old,
and a large grab handle was mounted on it. The ventilation system
was extended with two large rectangular vents mounted under the
centre of the dash. The steering wheel was modified so that the
whole width of the horizontal spoke was padded, rather in the
manner of the 99. The 96 had its back seat modified in the manner of

the 99. Previously it had been possible to extend the boot of the 96 by removing the rear seat, but removing the back seat had never been easy and there was the problem of what to do with the cushions when they had been removed; in addition to this the space was rather limited in its usefulness as it did not extend the load floor at all. The redesigned arrangement made full use of the potential of the idea. The horizontal squab pivoted forward to sit vertically behind the front seats, and after a clip had been released the vertical squab, hinged at the bottom, would fold forward to the horizontal, thus becoming part of the load floor and extending it by about 60 per cent. For the Swedish market rear shoulder belts had become standard. The exhaust system had been aluminiumised to make it more durable. Sadly the much loved V4 De Luxe model was no longer available. There was another change in the interior trim in 1970: the door and side panels became colour matched with and constructed in the same material as the seat sides.

The 1970 Rally Season

There was only one works car entered in the 1970 Monte Carlo, a fuel-injected V4 driven by Haken Lindberg and Arne Hertz. The car started well, but soon began to have braking problems—it didn't when it should have done. This got so bad that they coasted out of the rally. The problem was later traced to dirt in the hydraulics. Most of the cars in the Swedish rally suffered some form of misfortune as well. All the works cars were to Group 2 specification: Haken Lindberg, Carl Orrenius and Tom Trana having fuel-injection cars, Stig Blomqvist and Per Eklund having cars fitted with twin Webers. There had been a minor miscalculation and Per's car had received the wrong carburettor jets, which made the performance something like a standard two stroke. As soon as possible the carburettors, manifolds and cylinder heads were changed, but the temperature gauge connection was left off and the car overheated when snow blocked the radiator. This caused the cylinder-head gasket to blow and put Per out of the rally. Tom Trana had to retire on Special Stage 11 when his car dropped a valve, and Carl Orrenius retired on Special Stage 16 when a piston seized. Haken Lindberg's throttle linkage came adrift and he dropped to fourth position; in his attempt to pull back he rolled on Special Stage 17. This did not greatly affect him and he carried on, only to retire through transmission failure on Special Stage 35. Only Stig Blomqvist managed to emerge relatively unscathed and gain second place overall.

In the Italian Rally Tom Trana was fourth and Haken Lindberg was eighth. He would have been higher but he lost time having an engine mounting replaced. No official team was entered in the East Africa Safari, but a locally entered Saab came thirteenth. It was found that even before the start of the Austrian Alpine that Haken Lindberg's car had seized a piston ring. The mechanics ran it all night with the petrol heavily laced with upper-cylinder lubricant. In the morning the car ran, but made horrible noises. Eventually, after an otherwise uneventful drive, Haken brought the car into second place. Carl Orrenius was not so lucky: early in the rally his fan shot through the radiator, causing him to lose time, but not putting him out of the rally. He then broke a drive shaft when too far from the service point to avoid being eliminated. The privately entered car of A. Robertson came tenth in the Scottish Rally.

The RAC was, as in previous years, something of a chapter of accidents. Stig Blomqvist started very well, quickly moving into first place. However, he misunderstood an arrow and took a wrong turning. He managed to get back on the road fairly quickly, but was so angry that he went off the road again and lost ten minutes. At Blackpool he was lying fifth, and was climbing back up towards first place quite well until the final stage when he hit a wall and destroyed his gearbox. The rest of the team fared no better. Carl Orrenius in the only fuel-injected car retired with a broken drive shaft, Haken Lindberg retired when a pinion sheared in the gearbox and he was lying fourth. Tom Trana retired in Northumberland when the gearbox was reported to have 'blown up'. A private entrant, Joan Pink, put her Saab into a Scottish river. In all, not a particularly auspicious rally for Saab, although Lars Jonsson gained a very creditable ninth overall in a privately entered car.

Saab won the Norwegian Winter Rally and the Sorland Rally.

The 99 Model Range

In the spring of 1970 three new 99 models* were introduced, making four in all. Most interesting was the introduction of a four-door version of the car, this being the first four-door car Saab had ever produced. It was exactly the same size as the two-door model, but obviously the front doors were rather smaller in order to accommodate rear doors of a reasonable size. The doors were very well laid out in so far as they both were as large as possible, and as large as necessary, and the rear door made access particularly easy because the trailing edge of the doorway followed exactly the contour of the rear seat. Surprisingly enough the styling of the car came off well with four doors—not quite as pleasing to the eye as the two-door version, but not too different. The other two versions of the 99 also represented new ground for Saab in several ways. They were fully automatic versions of both the two- and four-door cars, Saab's first fully automatic cars having Borg-Warner three-speed automatic gearboxes. To compensate for the power loss resulting from the torque converter, automatic cars were fitted with the then modern Bosch D-Jetronic fuel-injection system, quite a complex electronic system complete with computer box. This gave 87 bhp compared with the carburettor version's 80 bhp. These figures were given at 5,500 rpm and 5,200 rpm respectively, and gave the automatic version performance on a par with the manual version—a most unusual but desirable situation. With the addition of these cars it became obvious that Saab were using the 99 to build up a range of quality family cars and push themselves up-market quite quickly. On the home market Volvo was the obvious target, and this range of four cars seemed to cover the 142 and 144 markets quite neatly.

For 1971 the model line-up was doubled to eight 99s. This came about with the introduction of a new engine—the 1709 cc engine had its bore increased to 87 mm which, retaining the stroke of 78 mm, gave a capacity of 1854 cc. This was the engine Triumph were to use in their Dolomite a year later. It is interesting to compare the details of the two engines. Those for the Triumph are in parentheses. Single Stromberg carburettor (twin Stromberg carburettors),

---

*Model means look, style, pattern; differing engine patterns did not create new models, just alternative variants of the same model.

The 1963 Monte Carlo Rally weather conditions were ideal for Saab's victory.

The 1956 Saab Sonett Super Sport, a lightweight sports car design based on the 93. This was partly a personal project on behalf of the designer, Rolfe Mellde, and partly to prove to the world that Saab could produce a sports car.

Stig Blomquist in the 1979
Circuit of Ireland driving a
Saab 2-door Turbo. Although
plagued with braking problems
on this event, he came first in
the Mintex Rally.

Above and below: Prototype of the Saab Sonett II. Designed by Sixten Sason, it utilised the floorpan and underbody of the Saab 96.

The prototype of the Saab Sonett II designed by Bjorn Karlstrom which was chosen for production. The car made its first public appearance in February, 1965 and went into production at the end of 1966.

The 1967 Saab Sonett II. It was destined almost exclusively for the American market where it was quite a success.

The early Saab Sonett facia.

The 1967 Saab Sonett II.

The 1968 Saab Sonett V4. The V4 was no faster than the old two-stroke model. However it could exceed 100 m.p.h. and was surprisingly economical, helped by a very low drag factor of only 0.32. A total of 1,610 V4s were produced.

The Saab Sonett III. There were many design changes made, including a tailgate and front end styling.

1974 Saab Sonett III. The Sonett I
than the Sonett II. The headlights
bumpers from the 99 added to meet

Longitudinal section of a two-
cylinder 28 horsepower engine.

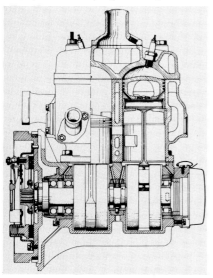

Longitudinal section of a three-
cylinder 40 horsepower engine.

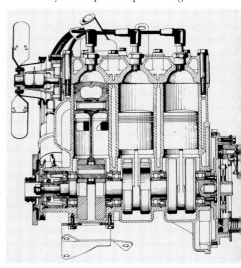

...ger in overall length but looked sleeker
...ed under flaps. The 74 model also had
...an safety regulations.

An earlier English-built 99 engine.

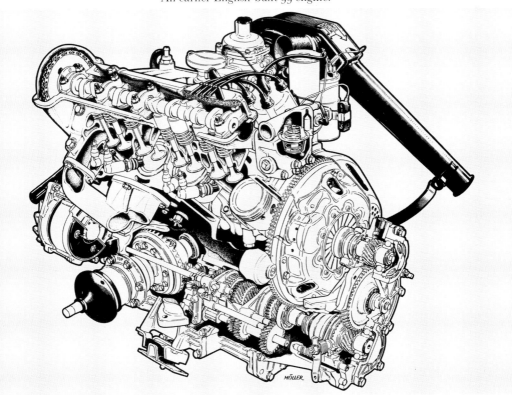

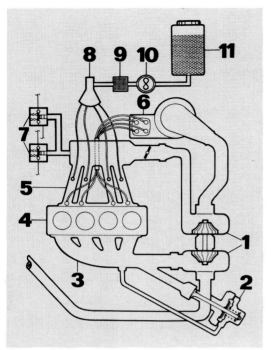

1. Turbocharger
2. Boost pressure control (waste-gate)
3. Exhaust manifold
4. Engine block
5. Intake branches
6. Air-fuel metering unit
7. Pressure guards
8. Magnetic valve with distribution chamber
9. Filter
10. High pressure pump
11. Water reservoir

The Saab Super Turbo – experimental car.
Schematic diagram of Saab Turbo engine with water injection.

A later Swedish-built 99 engine.

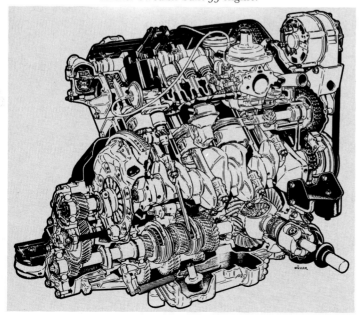

The 1965 Paddan – note widened body.

The Saab 99 represented a positive movement away from previous Saabs, yet shared many of the attributes of the earlier cars. This marked the start of their movement up-market. For the first year of production only one basic model was offered—the two-door saloon with a 1709 cc engine and a manual gearbox.

The 99 engine compartment.

Cutaway of the 1974 Saab 99.

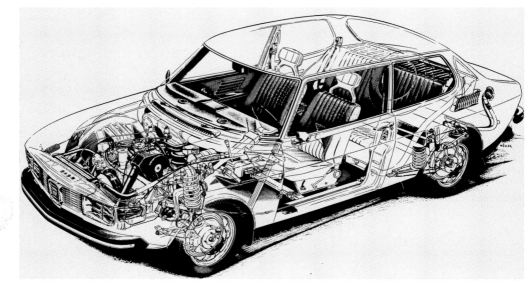

88 bhp at 5,000 rpm (91 bhp at 5,200 rpm), 109 lb ft at 3,000 rpm (105 lb ft at 3,500 rpm). So in actual fact the two engines were rather different in their methods of delivering power. This new engine was available in its carburettor form with a manual gearbox, the 1·7 engine remained an option. With an automatic gearbox the options were the 1·85 engine in either carburettor form or with the Bosch D-Jetronic system producing 95 bhp. This went someway towards answering the criticisms of the uninspiring performance of the 1·7 car. Although it did not really increase top speed its effects were felt particularly in improved top-gear acceleration. With the coming of the 1·85 engine the freewheel departed: its role in the 99 had always been somewhat anomalous. It was felt that with the higher torque of the larger engine the taking up of the slack would have a damaging effect on the gearbox. The most obvious external change to the car was the fitting of two small grilles below the main grille. This was to improve cooling with the larger engine, particularly gearbox cooling. The brakes and the ventilation system were also improved. The old fascia, good in itself, was replaced by a superb new one. The whole thing was moulded in a dense impact-absorbing foam, backed by deformable steel. This meant that in the event of an accident and an occupant of the car hitting the dash with some force it would deform, but slowly so that it would bring the person to a halt without too much damage being done. The structure was finished in a black leathercloth, similar to that on the V4 cars. Directly in front of the driver were three round instruments, quite considerably recessed into the dash. As on the old panel the central instrument was the speedometer. It was a more modern and slightly clearer design than the old one, and incorporated a trip distance recorder. To the right of the speedometer was a large clock, which replaced the rectangular central clock of the old model. To the left of the speedometer was a combination dial containing temperature gauge and fuel gauge. This was arranged in a completely different manner to the earlier dial: the gauges were placed to the left and right of the dial with the actual scales vertically parallel in the centre of the dial, with the pointers pivoting near the edges. This meant that both gauges could be read at a single glance. The temperature gauge was particularly easy to read for if the pointer was not horizontal there was something wrong. This dial also incorporated warning lights for full headlamp beam, indicators, brakes, low fuel, oil and charge. The

centre section of the fascia was given over to the controls for the heating and ventilation systems, basically three simple twist controls under which were two rectangular vents, and above which was a small shaped tray within reach of the seat-belted driver and suitable for a packet of cigarettes or similar objects. In front of the passenger was a large lidded glove compartment and at each end of the fascia were further air vents, each with individual controls. Below the section of the fascia described was a strip of polished wood, slightly angled upwards, on which those switches not mounted on the steering column were placed. Below this was a narrow strip of padding on which was mounted a large grab handle at the passenger side. Below this in the centre of the fascia was a pull-down ashtray which incorporated a cigarette lighter. The new fascia was very good and earned Saab a great deal of praise, as it broke new ground in terms of safety. Even the strip of wood which really should not have fitted in did not cheapen the whole effect and served the useful purpose of setting off the black rocker switches mounted on it, thus making them easier to see. It also broke the monotony of the black. The inside mirror was replaced by one of the dipping variety, given an anti-glare treatment.

The changes to the 95 and 96 for that year included the deletion of the bright strips on the wings which had characterised the cars since 1954. These were replaced by a single side moulding running along the bottom of the door and rear quarter panel. These were rather in the style of the old Sport or De Luxe models, but as they were mounted on rubber they went further towards protecting the car from minor impacts. The capping of the bottom of the leading edge of the rear wing became ridged black plastic, and the front piece of the strip incorporated a Saab logo. The handbrake lever was changed to make it neater in appearance and easier to use. The 95 gained more interior safety padding and a new seating arrangement—it became possible for the rear row of seats to be in use, while the centre row were down, so that a load could be carried in their place. This raised the number of possible seating arrangements to four.

Two important changes were made to all Saab models that year. The first involved rust protection and the introduction of Electrodip priming. This meant that, after phosphating in the usual way, the whole body would be lowered into a bath of electrodip primer and a strong electric current would be switched on to make the paint adhere to the entire surface of the car. This was particularly effective for coating hidden cavities, which probably would have escaped hand-spraying, and for coating the edges of the panels. The other innovation was another Saab 'world first'—headlamp washers and wipers. Many roads in Sweden, Norway and Finland were of rather doubtful quality, and in the winter they were particularly dirty, especially the many rural roads not properly made up. Tests had shown that headlamps were particularly prone to all mud thrown up, and that they would quickly lose up to 90 per cent of their efficiency in these conditions. Obviously in winter, when the headlamps were most needed they would get most dirty because of all the slush and salt on the roads. For some time Saab had been working on ideas to keep headlights clean, and the system they finally brought out consisted of a wiper blade which wiped horizontally from the inner side of the headlamp rim—the headlamp rim on the 95 and 96 had to be redesigned to accommodate them. The wiper was assisted by a washer jet which sprayed horizontally over the whole headlamp. The system was connected through the windscreen washer and wiper system, the headlamp washers and wipers being turned on when the windscreen washers were used. The headlamp wipers were also turned on when the windscreen wipers were on at their fastest speed. The headlamp washers and wipers were standard on all the models on the Scandinavian markets and on most of the other European markets. On other markets, for example Britain, they were optional. In America, because of the use of round headlights, they were not available at all. The wipers proved to be very successful, and won the gold medal of the Swedish Motormannens Riksforbund for Saab in 1971. The system had a great influence on the Swedish government as within a fairly short time they introduced legislation on the subject. Today headlamp washers and wipers have to be fitted to all new cars sold in Sweden.

The 1971 Rally Season

Stig Blomqvist was absolutely unstoppable in the 1971 Swedish Rally. He took the lead very early on and kept it for the rest of the rally. Tom Trana was tenth and Stenstrom was fifteenth. Carl Orrenius was excluded for 'dangerous practising'. There were no Saabs in the

Italian Rally, but two in the East Africa Safari. Saabs were being sponsored to enter the rally by the American firm Sears & Roebuck. Stig Blomqvist drove one car and Tom Trana was supposed to drive the other. However, he was ill and his place had to be taken by the top works mechanic Melin. Stig finished thirteenth in the rally. In March, in the Nordic Cup, Stig was first and Per Eklund was second.

Saabs from both Norway and Sweden were entered in the 1,000 Lakes, with Per and Stig driving the Swedish cars. Per had problems with his piston rings, which slowed him considerably, and necessitated a new set of plugs at the end of each stage. After a reasonable start Stig took the lead and kept it. The Finnish Saabs were rather unlucky, with Grondahl destroying his engine and Ultrainen breaking his petrol-pump drive. Per was seventh. In the TAP Carl Orrenius was forced to retire with a broken differential. Stig was going very well but had to change a wheel halfway through a special stage. Whilst doing this he managed to lose all the wheel bolts—quite an amazing achievement. Having done this he had no alternative but to finish the stage on three wheels. The damage he had done to the car took 52 minutes to repair, and he soon found himself out of time on the later stages.

The RAC Rally was very snowy, and perhaps this was the reason for the remarkable number of cars that hit things. Per Eklund started the trend when he hit a rock and broke a king pin. Notwithstanding this, Saab as a team was leading at the halfway mark, and Stig was personally leading the rally. Tordoff began the second half by shearing a shaft in his gearbox. Olle Dahl drove the car off the road at a bridge, but soon got it back on the road again. Ultrainen hit a rock and damaged his steering, and Per hit another rock, this time damaging his wheel bearing and stub axle. Not to be outdone Stig hit a deer near Carlisle, but only succeeded in damaging a few lights. However, all these inconveniently placed rocks and deer did not stop Saab picking up the team prize. With Stig first overall, Carl Orrenius third, Per Eklund seventh, Ultrainen tenth and Olle Dahl fifteenth. In all, quite an exceptional result.

Saab were runners-up in the manufacturers' championship and were also first overall in the KAK Rally, the Hankiralli, the Norwegian Winter Rally, the International Police Rally and in the 1,000 Lakes Rally.

Safety

Saab, throughout the period they have built cars, have had a philosophy of safety. Obviously this has come greatly to the fore in recent years now that safety has become an important issue, particularly in Scandinavia and the United States. This would seem to have accelerated Saab's development towards safer cars, but that is not to say that it was lacking before, as Saab have always been making safe cars, and were putting extra safety devices into their cars when nobody else was. This makes it interesting, and important, to look into Saab's philosophy of safety and to trace its development. Saab divide safety into two categories: primary, or active, safety, which is avoiding accidents; and secondary, or passive, safety, which is surviving accidents if they do happen. To consider primary safety, the most obvious theme that has run through all Saab cars is that of front-wheel drive. Saab committed themselves to it when very few cars used it, the two springing most immediately to mind being the Citroen and the DKW. This use of front-wheel drive was therefore quite a risky move for a firm with an unproven car who wanted to gain a place in a market suspicious of technical innovation. Saab justified this by their belief in the intrinsic superiority of front-wheel drive over rear-wheel drive in terms of control of the car and therefore safety. This soon became obvious in Sweden, where the Saab proved itself to be much safer in slippery conditions. Having the weight of the engine over the driven wheel helped traction enormously, and the car showed almost no tendency to skid. Any slight loss of traction would be at the front and could easily be righted by easing off the throttle a little, whereas on a front-engine, rear-wheel-drive car any loss of traction would almost certainly show itself at much lower speeds as a tail slide, very difficult and often impossible to correct. This made front-wheel drive intrinsically safer in slippery conditions. They also display far better road manners than rear-wheel-drive cars. The car's natural tendency on corners is to understeer. This is basically safe as it allows the driver to compensate slightly without risking strange reactions from the car. A rear-wheel-drive car is far more sensitive to loading to determine the way in which it handles, and in certain situations can display oversteering characteristics which can be very difficult to cure. So front-wheel

101

drive is more predictable than rear-wheel. The main criticisms of front-wheel drive tend to centre on the torque reaction which displays itself as a self centring effect on the steering with the power on. This is true but is not necessarily a bad fault, as it gives the driver an awareness of the road, and makes him drive the car rather than be driven by it. In any case this torque reaction is largely absent from later cars, especially the 99 range, because of much improved design of the front geometry.

Steering is very important in primary safety. It must be accurate and quick so that fast manoeuvres may be carried through with confidence. This leaves no room for any 'sponge' or slack. The obvious system was rack and pinion, always used by Saab, and always resulting in taut and accurate steering. This has to a certain extent been at the expense of rather heavy steering at low speed, which has characterised all pre-900 Saabs. The firm considers this a small price to pay for safe and accurate steering at speed. Suspension is equally important in the car's handling and roadholding qualities. Since 1955 and the introduction of the 93, Saabs have had coil springs all round, independent at the front, coupled with the slightly unusual arrangement of the back axle—lightweight and slightly U-shaped. This low unsprung weight has made the rear of the car very neutral, and thus accentuated the benefits of front-wheel drive, so that the tail always follows the direction of the nose, rather than breaking out on its own line. The suspension tends towards firmness in order to minimise body roll, but careful design and the use of good-quality telescopic shock absorbers on all models, except the rear of the 95, have kept ride comfort good. Sadly the suspension of the 92 was less of a success, but it was a good try, and at least they had the sense to put it right, rather than persevere with it. The suspension on the 92 must be put in context, because while it was far from perfect it was rather better than most systems around in the early 1950s. The front-engine, front-wheel-drive layout gave by far the best lateral stability in sidewinds with the weight of the engine over the driving wheels. The second criticism of the front-wheel-drive layout is that traction up steep hills is inferior to that of the rear-wheel-drive car because of the weight transfer from front to back wheels. In actual fact this is true only with the car heavily laden, and in these circumstances the front-wheel-drive car is likely to retain more positive steering as the percentage of the car's weight remaining on the front wheels will be greater.

Efficient and reliable brakes are necessary for effective primary safety. All Saabs have had hydraulic brakes. When the 92 was being designed mechanical brakes were still much in evidence. Saab never fitted them to their cars as they quite rightly considered them to be unreliable and inefficient. The early Saab system of drums all round was a fine system which, given a good push on the pedal, would stop the car quickly and safely with remarkably little drama. Constant development of the brakes kept them generally ahead of the rest of the industry—they were early in the fitment of a pressure-limiting valve to the rear of the 96 to prevent the rear brakes locking; first to fit diagonally split circuits; early in the fitment of front discs. The system fitted to the 99 was excellent, being the culmination of twenty years of development. It consisted of four-wheel disc brakes, with a servo, which did not lighten the weight of the brakes excessively. The brakes could easily give 1 g deceleration, without too much pressure being required. The handbrake was the most remarkable new feature of the 99: it acted on separate drums on the front wheels. Saab considered that front handbrakes were safer than rear ones as they left the driver with more chance of pulling up in a straight line without locking the wheels in an emergency stop. *Motor*, in their road test of a 99 in November 1969, recorded a figure of 0·7 g for the handbrake deceleration. This was probably a figure without precedent, and about twice as good as a normal handbrake (not much good for handbrake turns, though). As *Motor* commented: 'In effect, then, the car has three effective independent braking systems—belt, braces and string.'

Adequate performance and ease of control are also necessary for safety, and although the two-stroke cars do not look very fast on paper, by the standards of the 1970s, they had more than enough power to keep up with cars twice and three times their size in their day, and still retained a vital 'get you out of trouble' margin of power. Indeed, they are still eminently suitable for use on the road today. The V4 quite simply is almost impossible to fault in terms of performance. Perhaps this is best illustrated by the fact that Saab have felt no need to change the engine's output since its introduction in 1966. Whilst the early 99s had no sporting pretensions they were by no means slow, and later 99s are dealt with elsewhere. Interior comfort and layout of controls, again vital for primary safety, are dealt with in greater detail elsewhere.

Visibility has never been a forte of Saab—they have always tended to see large windows as points of structural weakness, and their commitment to aerodynamics has always precluded sharp, easily seen, extremities. The 92 was the worst offender. Rearward visibility was very poor because of the sloping tail and small rear window. Saab cannot be condemned too much for this as visibility was not considered much by any manufacturer at that time, and the very small budget meant they could not afford large expanses of glass. The 93 was not notably better, although the area of glass was somewhat larger. A real advance came with the 95 and 96, which, whilst not perfect, were a great improvement. The estate body of the 95 lent itself particularly to good rearward visibility, and the rear window on the 96 probably provided the best solution within the possibilities offered by the body. The fact that Saab were conscious that visibility was still not perfect is emphasised by the enlargement of the windscreen and 96 rear window in 1968. The 99 was always good in terms of visibility. The windscreen was remarkably large and, being curved, offered an almost unprecedented field of view. Although sometimes criticised for high waistline, rearwards or sideways vision has never been criticised, though the question of headrests will be dealt with later. Saabs have always had good electric wipers, windscreen washers since 1958, and throughout their history have recognised that lights are for seeing and being seen. The lights at the rear of the 92, although pitifully small by today's standards, were large by the standards of 1950, and the headlamps were powerful, although not immune from the rusting of reflectors that seems to beset all non-sealed-beam units. The lights have been progressively enlarged and improved since, and in the 1970s Saab have probably led the way in this field. Although it might be said that in the 1960s they did retain the single-lensed rear lights, serving a multiplicity of functions, for a little too long and, going further back, semaphore direction indicators were never ideal.

In terms of secondary safety, all Saabs have been famous for their strength. The 92 was one of the strongest cars ever made, significantly stronger than the 99, in itself a very strong car. Of course as the 92 had a very small window and no bootlid it was bound to be strong. The car illustrates the structural strength that can be obtained with good design and unitary construction. Naturally rallying has tested the strength of the cars, not least for the reason that rally drivers tend to run into trees, boulders, cliffs and other similar wayside objects. It is fair to say that the Saab offers a greater chance of survival under these circumstances than almost any other car of its period. The built-in roll cage has always been a Saab feature, the unitary construction of the car being complemented by a framework of rigid and heavy steel sections, further strengthened by the windscreen and side pillars incorporating further and heavier steel strengthening. Thus, from the very beginning, Saabs incorporated a rigid passenger compartment with deformable sections front and rear, many years before the rest of the motor industry considered them. One of the tests the factory submits the cars to is to drop them on to their roofs from 2 metres on to concrete—the cars do not collapse and the damage to the roof is merely superficial denting of panels rather than structural deformation. They also came well out of the test in which they are driven into a concrete wall, showing no damage behind the bulkhead between the engine and passenger compartments. The most spectacular display of Saab strength came in February 1962 when, for a Swedish television programme on safety, Arne Ingier drove a Saab 96 off the top of a ski jump near Oslo. The car fell with considerable impact and rolled over quite a number of times before coming to a halt on its wheels. It was very lightly damaged in terms of its panels and structurally unscathed. Arne Ingier then drove the car away.

Two more vital secondary safety features in Saabs are the position of the steering box and of the petrol tank. The steering box has always been put at the back of the engine compartment in a shielded position to protect it from all but the very worst frontal impacts. This means that, in the event of accident, the driver retains as much control of the car as possible. In all Saabs except the 92 the petrol tank has been placed between the back wheels, away from the very tail of the car and also within the body, thus protected by the floor-pan. On the 96, the petrol tank is placed under the boot floor, ahead of the spare wheel, thus protected from impact at all angles. The arrangement is similar on the 93, 95 and 99. Unfortunately the arrangement on the 92 was slightly less safe: the tank was in the point of the tail of the car, and subject to damage from any tail impact. An error, though not an uncommon one at that time, that was rectified reasonably quickly and in Saab's defence it must be said that the positioning of the petrol tank was never easy without a bootlid, luggage being loaded from within the car. The work of protecting occupants from injury in the interior of the car has been chronicled elsewhere. Suffice it to say the rest of the motor industry lagged behind. Seatbelts were fitted at an early point and, before that, seatbelt mounting points. The interior mirror has always been framed and would always break off on impact.

Saab's commitment to safety took another step forward in 1971 with the establishment of the Road Accident Investigation Group. This group was set up by the company in order to study more serious accidents to Saabs. In general it took the cars that had been written off and, as well as examining the cars, interviewed the people directly involved—witnesses, police, doctors and the like—and examined reports and medical records. In all, about twenty-four man hours were spent on each accident.

In addition to examining individual accidents, the group made a more general study of all accidents during the relevant period in order to confirm the statistical reliability of the detailed data. The conclusions that the group has come to have been directly incorporated into the design of Saabs in the 1970s, and have complemented the American and Scandinavian safety legislation, thus keeping Saab ahead of it. The conclusions drawn from the first phase of investigations showed the Saab designers that one of the easiest ways for the occupants of the car to be safer was for them to wear seatbelts—the risk of injury was almost twice as great when they were not used and the type of injury far more serious. This worried the designers, because the wearing of seat belts was a thing over which they had little control—they could do no more than make the seatbelts as convenient and comfortable as possible, perhaps adding signs on the fascia.

It may be seen therefore that Saab's commitment to safety goes further than merely adding safety extras when the market demands it. They have made safety part of their philosophy of building cars, essential to all their planning. They have led the way in safety features and in many respects are much more advanced than the much acclaimed Volvo. Certainly in the field of primary safety they are way ahead, for the Volvo has never been known for quick accurate handling or electrifying performance. In terms of secondary safety, many features that Volvo have proclaimed in recent years have been on Saabs, unheralded, for many years.

Saab have not wholeheartedly welcomed all new US safety legislation, as they view much of it as being on the wrong track and not suited to European needs. For instance, American legislation concentrates on strengthening of the body too much, relying almost entirely on barrier tests, which are only limited in relevance. When considering side impacts the Americans legislate on strengthening doors. Saab, with their road-accident investigation group, have discovered that most people injured in side impacts are not crushed, but hurt by being thrown against the car interior. Thus priority should be on extra interior padding, rather than extra structural strength.

American exhaust emission regulations forced a change of engine size upon the V4 Saabs destined for the American market in the autumn of 1970. The engine was increased in capacity to 1·7 litres. As compression ratio was lowered to 8:1 the output remained at 65 bhp. It was a considerably cleaner engine. The big change was the introduction of a heated driver's seat. This was completely new—no manufacturer had ever offered one before. The seat had been developed for two basic reasons: first to improve the health of the driver—for it was considered that a cold seat was responsible for a number of back ailments; second, and more important, it improved safety for in a cold car on a cold seat the driver is less at ease and cannot concentrate properly on driving. Thus Saab carefully developed a heated seat. Temperature was fixed only after extensive surveys to decide at what temperature people felt chilly, and at what temperature they felt comfortable. The different designs of heating elements had been subjected to cold-room tests, impact tests, water-saturation tests and long-term overheating tests before a final design was arrived at. This consisted of net pouches containing four sets of heating wires on a reflective background. One pouch was placed under the surface of the seat, and another under the surface of the backrest. A thermostat was placed near the surface of the seat and this switched the heating elements on at temperatures below 14°C (57°F), and switched them off at 27·5°C (82°F).

Other changes common to all models included new road wheels. Instead of the old round perforations there were rectangular holes, angled towards the wheel rim. This was not to improve the appearance of the wheel but to improve braking. The old wheels had been designed for drum brakes and tended to throw rather too much dirt over the disc brakes for them to retain efficiency in the long run. The new wheels retained the good cooling of the old wheels, but kept the disc appreciably cleaner. The springs were uprated all round the 99 and, at the front of the 95 and 96, the shock absorber ratings were adjusted in keeping with this. This change was to make the handling on the 99 slightly more taut and to make all of the cars less subject to bottoming than before—though the claim that it provided an overall improvement in ride comfort does seem a little far-fetched. Other changes common to all models included new locks, with the key returning automatically to the neutral position and new rear mudflaps with the simpler Saab logo, rather than the old aeroplane symbol. The 95 and 96 received new overriders moulded in black rubber, although the rear of the 95 retained the old overriders. The new ones made parking bumps far less damaging. A 1972 V4 may be told from a 1971 model with one's eyes shut. The old exhaust note, with its slightly uneven beat caused by the fact that the pipes leading from each block to the front silencer were of unequal length, was rather unpopular and out of step with Saab's updated image. Hence the two pipes were made equal in length and the 1972 V4s acquired a more pleasant exhaust note.

The greatest change to the 99 concerned the bumpers. They had been prepared over quite a considerable time to conform with the projected US safety legislation relating to deformable bumpers. Saab wanted a neat bumper which did not necessitate the car being altered, except for minor local strengthening. A straight bumper was rejected because, if it was strong enough to take an impact anywhere along its length, it would have been too strong for the barrier tests and cause high decelerations. The final bumper curved out to a central point which would take the first impact and absorb it along its whole length rather than at a single point. Thus deceleration would be more gradual. The construction of the bumper was unique. Its basis is the slightly curved, heavy channel-shaped steel beam. On this are mounted blocks of cellular plastic sheathed in rubber. These blocks have rather the appearance of a honeycomb, and are the impact-absorbing part of the bumper. Finally there is a further heavy black sheathing, bound with a decorative bright metal strip. The mountings in the car were strengthened. The result of this development was a neat and compact bumper which could absorb impacts of up to 5 mph without sustaining permanent damage and if damaged at higher speeds single cellular blocks could be cheaply replaced. If anything it improved the look of the 99, giving it an air of robustness and quality (which is more than can be said of the less elegant offerings from such as Volvo and MG). The bumpers were rather larger than the old ones and mounted rather higher and this necessitated various other changes. The two separate air-intake apertures were covered by the new bumper and therefore their covering grilles were deleted. The old indicator/sidelamp cluster would have been obscured and so was replaced by a much larger cluster on the wings by the headlamps, bringing the design much more in line with the V4s. The new bumper also covered the old mounting for the twin horns, so these were replaced by a single horn mounted inside the engine compartment and for good measure the twin horns on the 95 and 96 were replaced by single units. That the new bumper covered the cooling apertures caused a deterioration in engine cooling and this necessitated fitting a larger-size fan and increasing the capacity of the fan motor to 150 watts. The radiator was moved forward at the same time, giving more under-bonnet space. A neat touch to the new front bumper was the provision of mountings for spotlights, with wires already running to them. On the subject of wiring, the system on all the models was simplified. The 1·7 litre engine was deleted and the only engine available was the 1·85 unit. This was available in either carburettor or injection form on both manual and automatic cars. The output of each version had been raised by 2 bhp.

The 99 EMS

Early 1972 saw a new version of the 99 introduced—the 99 EMS. The EMS stood for Electronic Manual Special. The car was available only in two-door, manual-transmission form, with the new Swedish built 2 litre engine. The car looked distinctive—having the very smart Saab alloy wheels fitted to it and being finished only in metallic paint. The grille was black with single chrome horizontal strip. Inside, the front seats had headrests, the steering wheel was smaller in diameter and had a padded leather rim and the larger clock was replaced by a tachometer, which had a small clock inset. The suspension was uprated. Without doubt the car was highly desirable as a fast and more exclusive Saab. Perhaps also this car may be seen as Saab's first real attempt to cash in on the lucrative market of the two-door BMWs. If this was so the EMS provided a good start, but was distinctly underpowered for this section of the market. The appearance of the EMS thus divided the 99 range in two degrees of luxury. The normal 99s, two- and four-door and the deluxe sports 99 EMS two-door.

The 1972 Rally Season

There were no works Saabs in the 1972 Monte Carlo Rally, though a private entrant did manage to come thirtieth overall. The Arctic Rally was cursed by distributor-drive problems. Simo Lampinen retired first with a sheared distributor drive. Ultrainen retired with a holed piston; Valkas had his distributor drive shear, which was replaced, only for him to retire with a cracked block. Lehtonen had his distributor drive shear but he finished fifth and another Saab was ninth.

In the Swedish there were works cars for Stig Blomqvist, Carl Orrenius, Per Eklund and Ake Andersson. Carl lasted a very short time, breaking his gearbox on the first stage and having to retire. Per had to have his petrol tank changed on a road section because of a blockage and this cost him two minutes. Stig made a very good start and was quite well ahead. Ake had a wheel fall off the back of his car, and so had to finish the stage on three wheels—he lost time at the end of the stage having his axle changed. Tordoff lost direct drive and so he had to use freewheel. Unfortunately his freewheel broke and he was forced to retire. Per blew a head gasket. Stig continued his immaculate performance and won the rally, with Per eighth and, as there were also Saabs in eighteenth and nineteenth positions, they were second in the team award. A locally entered Saab in the East Africa Safari was forced to retire without an exhaust system. In the Welsh Rally Bloxham in the *Birmingham Post*-sponsored V4 gained a very creditable fourth overall.

The Acropolis proved most unlucky for Saab. Stig started by going off the road on a very tricky tarmac/gravel bend on the first stage. He managed to get a tree stuck between the wheel and the front wing and lost eighteen minutes whilst being extricated. He made good times after this but finally had to retire with a broken gearbox. Per lost time with a blocked fuel line, which had to be disconnected from the tank and blown through. He later retired with a stripped crown wheel and pinion. Isrealson's car locked itself in freewheel, and then the starter motor failed. The car was impossible to start and he had to retire. Johansson was out of the time limit.

In the 1,000 Lakes Stig and Simo were in works Group 5 Saabs— stripped Group 2 cars—and Per was in an ordinary Group 2 car. The whole rally revolved around a three-cornered battle between Stig, Simo and Makinen. Stig lost some time on the fifth stage when he had to stop because he thought that his front suspension was damaged. In fact it was just a stone jammed in his disc. He still managed to be third fastest on this particular stage. Ultrainen snapped a wishbone and lost a front wheel, causing him to crash into a potato field. Stig was driving well, lost 100 points when caught in a radar trap, but was soon back in third place again. However, he had been driving with a little too much verve: having overrevved the engine he broke the crank and holed the sump. Amazingly he still managed to be first on this stage. Lehtonen had to drive the last three stages without any brakes at all as the fluid had mysteriously disappeared. Simo had driven very well throughout and had no problems. He came in first, with Per fifth and Lehtonen ninth and Saab won the team prize. The *Birmingham Post* Saab came sixth in the Burmah Rally.

In the Austrian Alpine Stig lost his brakes completely on one downhill section and did not bother to take the bend at the bottom. He damaged the car considerably and could not go on with the rally, but caused quite a sensation by driving up the Autobahn to Baden on three wheels. Per also lost his brakes and went off the track at a hairpin, but his car was less badly damaged and he continued, to finish third overall. The privately entered Saab of Ivarsson retired with a broken crank. In the Lindisfarne Rally Tordoff came fourth.

Stig and Per made a good start in the RAC, lying second and third in the early stages. The *Birmingham Post* Saab was an early retirement. Stig, although having hit some sheep, was still second at the halfway mark; Per was third, Lehtonen was twenty-third, and

Carl Orrenius was twenty-fourth. The second half was uneventful except for Per hitting a bridge and having to retire. The final placings were Stig second, Carl Orrenius thirteenth, Lehtonen fifteenth and Olle Dahl twenty-second.

Saab were also first overall in the KAK, the Hankiralli and the Jyv Skyl.

Reorganisation

In May 1972 the Saab—Scania Automotive Division was divided into the Saab Car Division and the Scania Division. The Saab Car Division headquarters was moved from Sodertalje to Nykoping, and a new engine plant for the 99 was built within existing buildings at Sodertalje. Having an engine built in Britain had distinct dis-advantages—modifications to it could only be done after negotiations with Triumph and were confined only to those that Triumph could, or would, do. Obviously in the long run, if major development was to take place to keep the engine in line with new Saab models, it was more desirable for Saab to build the engine themselves. The old 1·7 litre engine had been far from ideal, as the power-to-weight ratio of the car was not high enough. The 1·85 engine had been a great improvement, particularly in petrol-injection form, but it was obvious that the car would benefit greatly from a larger engine and 2 litres seemed ideal for the size of the car, and because most of the 99's competitors and prospective competitors—Peugeot 504, BMW 2002, Opel Rekord and the like—had engines of about that capacity. This therefore seemed a suitable moment for Saab to take over the production of the engine, especially as the Sodertalje plant gave them suitable premises and Triumph's development of a 2 litre from the 1·85 engine was moving along different lines—witness the 16 valve 'Sprint' engine.

Engine Development

The first thing that Saab did with the 1·85 was enlarge the distance between the cylinder axes. This made room for larger cylinder bores

—90 mm as against 87 mm—and a larger water jacket. The 78 mm stroke was retained. The single-row timing chain of the original engine was replaced by a duplex one, considered to be more durable. All this made the engine about 2 in longer. At the bottom the enlarged sump was utilised to make the main-bearing supports bigger. The cylinder head showed the most important differences between new and old engines. The old cylinder head had been a distinct compromise because of Triumph's desire to use the engine as a basis for a V8. The valves had been set in parallel and inclined in relation to the cylinders in order to reduce width of the canted engine. This was a very good idea in principal as it meant that any future V8 could be fitted into a relatively narrow engine house. However, it did have its disadvantages, centring on rather poor thermal efficiency. As Saab came to have no intention of building a V8 from the engine they had to suffer its disadvantages without benefiting from its advantages. They also had to suffer the rather strangely angled cylinder-head bolts that Triumph had insisted on. Therefore, on the new engine, the axes of the valves were in line with those of the cylinders, and the cylinder-head bolts went into the block vertically. The rocker cover was enlarged to cover them. With the valves no longer at an angle to the pistons, the wedge-shaped combustion chamber could be dropped, as it duly was. The new chambers were partly in the tops of the pistons, thus significantly improving thermal efficiency. The final modification was to put the alternator on a bracket on top of the timing cover, thus removing it from its close proximity to the exhaust manifold with the resultant heat build-up. The engine had the relatively low compression ratio of 8·7:1 (against 9:1 for the 1·85 engine). The 1985 cc engine was introduced in the EMS as a replacement for the 1854 cc. In this application it had the Bosch D-Jetronic injection and developed 110 bhp at 5,500 rpm and an even more creditable 123 lb ft of torque at 3,500 rpm. This provided improved performance and gave Saab the added bonus of easily passing all the US emission laws. The introduction of another version of the engine came in 1973, but not for the US market. This had a single Stromberg 175 CD carburettor and developed 95 bhp at 5,200 rpm, and 116 lb ft at 3,500 rpm. It seemed that Saab had the engines for the 99 that they wanted from the start. With these came another important advance.

The Line-Out System

For quite a considerable time it has been recognised that production-line assembly is not the best system for producing cars. Its social implications centre around the boredom caused by the repetitive nature of the job and the short working cycle. It was estimated that each operation done on the Saab production line took on average 1·8 minutes. This was not only bad for individual workers but also bad for the company in that turnover of skilled shop-floor workers was running annually at between 45 and 55 per cent in the early 1970s. Worse still from the point of view of production, absenteeism rose from 15 per cent in 1971 to 23 per cent in 1974 and showed no signs of abating. This, coupled with the fact that by the very nature of production-line work one man has one specific job to do and the whole line grinds to a halt if he does not do it, made it very difficult to build cars at all on some days.

Obviously a solution had to be found. Two possibilities presented themselves: first that incentive bonus schemes should be introduced to reward long service and regular attendance. This seemed to be a case of treating the symptoms rather than the disease, and it is doubtful that this sort of scheme would have been successful in maintaining low levels of absenteeism and worker turnover in the long term. It offered no solution to the social problems posed by production-line working, but merely sought to obscure the question. The second possibility offered a rather more adventurous solution: to dispense completely with production-line assembly. The Saab management, in co-operation with the workers, had for some time been examining alternatives to production-line working, and in 1972 they had the ideal opportunity for putting into practice the results of their work. This came with the opening of the Sodertalje works to make engines for the 99. Saab already felt that they had developed the production-line working system to its fullest extent. This was probably true. They had slowed the line to a relatively low speed as they calculated that whatever the speed of the line a man always takes the same amount of time to prepare for a given operation, so the faster the speed of the line the less time is actually productive. Additionally, quality is likely to suffer as speed increases. It was obvious that this did not provide an effective solution so it was decided to structure the new factory not on the production-line principle but on group assembly, or what has come to be known as 'line-out' working.

This system merits further study as it has become central to the construction of Saab cars. First the major engine components: the block is cast on the factory site, by a hot-box method, with the core sand being coated with resin to give it a hard surface. This gives a much cleaner and more accurate casting than the older method. The casting is then transported to the engine workshop for machining. This is largely done by automatic-transfer machines. The block goes through about eight operations, including inspection involving pressure testing to see that the blocks are not porous and a comprehensive dimensional check. The connecting rods are made by outside contractors but still have to undergo a similar process of machining and inspection to the blocks. Machining of the crankshaft is slightly different as it involves more manual setting-up than any other major parts, but where automation is possible it is employed. The cylinder heads are delivered unmachined, and are made of a light alloy—silumin. They are machined automatically, wet to dissipate the heat and to flush away the swarf. The machined components are then taken to the pre-assembly area, still structured in the form of a rectangular production line. Here the crankshaft, connecting rods and pistons are fitted to the block, the cylinder head is assembled and also fitted to the block. The part-assembled engine is then taken to the final assembly stations. It is here that the new system of group assembly is used. Fitters are divided into teams of three or four members, each group having an engine to assemble. This involves fitting the flywheel, carburettor or fuel-injection unit, distributor, sparking plugs, timing chain and everything else needed to make the engine ready for the car. The group is given thirty minutes and has to decide how the work is to be done. Normally there is some form of work rotation so that each group member becomes familiar with all the jobs involved. This maintains the interest of the worker, making his lot more pleasant, and it less likely that he will leave or go absent without good reason. It also means that when people are absent it is much easier to maintain production as everybody knows how to do all the jobs. When the engine has been assembled it is run for fifteen minutes before being put into the car. This system of line-out working has been very successful in reducing absenteeism and employee turnover, and has also improved quality and industrial relations. It is probably also true to say that it has led to a more contented and fulfilled workforce. Saab are presently extending the system to all the factories in which it is workable. They have already extended it into the 99 body-assembly area with larger groups, up to about six, and up to about an hour for each working cycle. Groups are gradually being allocated more responsibility and wider authority.

Saab are trying to involve the shop-floor worker in development work, as well as increasing his involvement in production work. With this aim in mind development groups have been established to supplement the production groups. These groups are basically concerned with the improvement of working methods and conditions. As a rule several production groups are attached to one development group, all sending representatives to it, and maintaining close contacts with it. Other representatives include management, engineers and, at times, outside experts. These development groups have made valuable contributions to the running of the factories, especially the Sodertalje plant. At the centre of worker–management co-operation lies the works council. This is a very well established body, originally set up thirty years ago to foster good relations and understanding between the workers and the management. It has not merely survived but prospered and become an integral part of the Saab–Scania structure. The council consists of representatives of all types of worker and the management. The council has forty representatives and holds six meetings per year. Eight members are elected to form the executive committee, which provides a sort of catalyst between the works council, the collaboration councils and the various committees. Its duties include preparing material for the works council and following up its decisions. The collaboration councils are the local works councils in different sections of the company. For example, transmission works, foundry, spare parts department, marketing section. These councils deal with everyday matters relating to their particular section, thus helping to reduce the work load of the works council. The committees are directly attached to the works council and deal with specific areas. There are at present nine committees which are permanent; temporary committees are sometimes formed to deal with pressing short-term problems. There are committees dealing with suggestions, personnel, rationalisation, recreation, environment, traffic, safety, energy supply and economy. This last committee is the newest and the most interesting as it breaks new ground in that it is formed to give employees a better insight into the running of the company. Saab–Scania are justifiably proud of their work in labour relations and new work methods. They have broken new ground in many fields and if they continue to progress along the same lines they seem set for a stable future in terms of labour relations.

Changes for 1973

In the spring of 1973 a 'price leader' for the 99 range was introduced in the form of the X7. This was mainly for the Danish market, where high import duties made the cars very expensive. The car was only available in two-door form with the 88 bhp engine and a manual gearbox. The car had the old chrome bumpers rather than the impact-absorbing ones. The car also had the older road wheels with round holes and no bright mouldings on the window frames. Inside it had the front seats of the 95/96 and trim that was generally slightly simpler than the other models. The basic models of the previous year were given the designation L. The two-door came as standard with the 88 bhp engine, but was available with the 2 litre engine in either carburettor or fuel-injection form, with either manual or automatic transmission. The four-door only was available with the 2 litre engine. The EMS remained at the top of the range in two-door petrol injection manual form only. For that year all 99s except the X7 and the American models were given H4 Halogen headlamp bulbs. The front springs were pivot-mounted at the bottom in order to keep the coil straight at all times and so at its most efficient. The steering-gear lubrication was changed from grease to oil—this had better low-temperature characteristics and made the steering slightly lighter at low speeds. All 99 grilles became black, and the EMS grille received an extra bright strip to keep it different. Hubcaps were altered slightly, as were certain badges. Sunvisors were improved and the instruments received fluorescent amber pointers. The road accident investigation group's findings were filtering through to the customer in the form of additional safety features. The group had discovered that many accidents were of the side-impact variety. Hence it was decided to strengthen the doors against side impacts. Heavy rectangular-section steel beams were welded longitudinally into the doors at the height to afford maximum protection for the passengers. At the same time a moulded fibreglass headlining was fitted to the car, insulating the passengers from temperature extremes and, more important, had great qualities of impact absorption; in the event of an accident it would protect the passengers from impact with the roof members. The headlining was, of course, fire resistant. The 1972 95/96 was continued unchanged for 1973.

The 1973 Rally Season

In the 1973 Arctic Rally Tapio Rainio came fourth, and Lehtonen received the doubtful honour of having a special prize for being the first car to roll over. The Swedish Rally was extremely competitive— to begin with studded tyres were not allowed—and lay completely between Stig and Per. After seven stages Stig was leading Per by five minutes, but Stig lost twelve minutes because of a faulty petrol pump. This put Per back into contention and the rest of the rally was hard fought between the two team-mates, with Stig finally just beating Per into second place. In the Austrian Alpine, Stig was lying second and just beginning to overtake the leading car when his differential failed and he had to retire. Per came second. Alistair Robertson came fifth in the Saltire Rally.

Stig retired in the RAC, in slightly strange circumstances, in Wales. He had hit something unidentified which caused the front wheel, both wishbones and their mounting points to be bent. He straightened things out with a jack and finished the stage, where further straightening-out continued. However, the vibration was still so bad that it shook the carburettors and the exhaust off and they ran out of time making repairs. Simo was also having problems: his car was not fitted with a head gasket, but an arrangement of sealing rings, these working only intermittently and causing a great thirst for water from time to time. At York they were fifth, just ahead of Per. By the Lake District they had moved up the field to lie just behind Clark. Per lost five minutes in a Scottish forest when he left the track. Simo's engine finally seized on the penultimate test—he managed to freewheel to the finish. They tried to restart the car by towing it, but this only broke the crankshaft and drove a con rod through the side of the block. Per broke a front wishbone on the final stage and was forced to retire.

In the Rally of 1,000 Lakes Simo lost his freewheel at a significant moment, and this caused him to go off the road. However, he got the car back on to the road and finished fourth. Per's car destroyed a remarkable number of drive shafts and he got so fed up with it that he retired on the last stage. Stig managed to get into the lead, but he blew up his engine trying to stay there. Saab did well in the other Scandinavian rallies, coming first and second in the KAK Rally, first and third in the Finnish Hankiralli and first, second and third in the Swedish Championship. They also came first in the Cyprus Rally.

Changes for 1974

The most noticeable change for the 95s and 96s in 1974 was the adoption of a new grille. The lines were the same as the old grille but it was made entirely out of plastic. It was basically black, to bring it in line with the rest of the Saab models, but the frame, the headlamp surrounds and the single horizontal bar were silver grey. Inertia-reel seatbelts became standard in Scandinavia and a seatbelt reminder light was also fitted. The interior was redesigned slightly with a heavier, more durable velour on the seats. Other changes included a larger windscreen-washer reservoir and a new radiator. The 99 also benefited from the internal improvements, indeed more so: the most obvious change was the new seats in the L and EMS models. The squab was retained little changed but the backrest was extended upwards to include an integral headrest. This involved total redesign of the seat frame so that the backrest was of even strength throughout its height. There can be no doubt that seats of this type protect the driver better in an accident, particularly from whiplash. It also seems likely that the extra comfort of the seats makes the driver more relaxed and so improves his driving. Unfortunately it is equally true to say that they can impair rearward vision and be slightly less than pleasant for those sitting behind them. Saab attempted to solve this problem by removing a section from the headrest part of the seat—so leaving a sort of 'window' in the seat. Certainly this was a good idea, and helped to a certain extent, but it still left the rear-seat passengers with a claustrophobic feeling. On the British market Saab have always encountered a certain amount of adverse reaction to the car because of this. The main seat facing was in velour, though the actual headrest was faced with plastic. The trim on the L was similar to that on the old seat, but the EMS received a new pattern. It also received a central rear armrest and new door and side panels. They were made of energy-absorbing polyurethane materials, covered in vinyl. They were another product of the research done by the road accident investigation group. It had been discovered that not only was greater side-impact protection needed, but also greater internal padding to protect passengers from being injured by being thrown against projections. Hence the impact-absorbing panels on the EMS (and the Combi). The L and EMS models received a new steering wheel, with a larger area of padding on it. The heater was improved, particularly in relation to rear-window demisting. Windscreen wipers were painted black, so as not to reflect and dazzle the driver. On certain models power steering became an option. This was particularly valuable as 165-section tyres replaced the 155-section tyres on the 2 litre model, this being hardly designed to improve the problem of low-speed heaviness of the steering. Unfortunately power steering could not be fitted to right-hand-drive cars. Externally the bumpers were a little stronger and had been moved away from the body. Common to 95/96 models and 99 models for 1974 was an improvement in anti-corrosion methods with a waxy oil being sprayed into all the box sections, and over the underside of the car.

The Combi Coupe

In 1974 a completely new model appeared on the Swedish roads, the Saab Combi Coupe. Saab were conscious that the 95 was getting old-fashioned and had rather a limited life. Therefore it was felt that some sort of estate car should be offered in the 99 range. First a conventional estate was designed and actually got to prototype stage before rejection. It is probably true to say that an obvious utility car in the range would adversely effect the executive-car image that Saab were trying to promote. The aim therefore became a vehicle with additional load-carrying capacity and a large rear door, but which did not actually look like an estate car. After some research it was decided that on a normal estate car the area to the rear of the car near to the roofline was seldom used. It was therefore decided to produce a car with this area deleted. The roofline of the Combi is exactly the same as that of the saloon, with the side window bearing as much family resemblance as possible. The car was designed by Bjorn Envall, who had been playing around with sketches for quite some time. The designs changed little, though some of the early ones tended to have a slightly concave line from the back of the roof to the top of the rear panel, reflecting the line of the saloon. However, this idea was soon abandoned and the final shape of the Combi soon emerged. The rear side window was slightly enlarged and the tailgate of the car was enormous—running from the trailing edge of the roofline to the bumper, it had a fairly large rear window and was raised by two gas-filled struts. The rear lights were totally new, being mounted on the corners of the car, square to the rear with a triangular section to the side, the light being visible from both the rear and the side. The side extractor vents were redesigned and finished with smaller black plastic grilles with 'Combi Coupe' in script on them. The petrol filler was moved to the other side of the car and given a round door. The rear seat folded down, and a parcel shelf could be slid in and out. The spare wheel was vertically mounted to the left of the luggage compartment. The rear overhang of the car had been lengthened by 110 mm and this was well used in the form of extra space. The space available was remarkably good: in the saloon with the back seat up, there was 347 litres of space available; in the Combi 381 litres. In the saloon with the back seat folded, there was 660 litres, whilst in the Combi there was 1,500 litres. Of course the rear of the car had to be extensively strengthened, as the third door left a very big hole. It is all credit to the engineers at Saab that the car was so little heavier than the two-door saloon.

The first prototypes were running late in 1971 and were then winter-tested. The final testing was done in 1972 and early 1973. The cars were very little different to drive from the saloons, though the weight distribution made the handling slightly inferior—though by too small a margin to be noticed. The car did not look quite as well balanced as the saloon, the length of the tail making the nose look rather short, but the car was by no means bad-looking. Saab announced the car as being something completely new, a Combi Coupe: a mixture of saloon, coupe and estate car, the only one of its type. This was not entirely true as certain cars were very close to it in both concept and execution. It is fairer to say that the car was one of the first really practical applications of the coupe/hatchback concept, and that it seemed to have established a trend.

The 1974 Rally Season

The wide selection of Saabs entered in the 1974 Arctic Rally was reflected by the number in the results. Rainio was first, Stig second, Simo fifth, Per sixth, Malmgren ninth and Petersson tenth. Not surprisingly they won the team award. The Monte Carlo Rally and the Swedish Rally were cancelled because of the oil crisis, as were a number of others.

In the 1,000 Lakes Simo rejetted his carburettor and removed his air filter in pursuit of more power. This was a mistake as he lost much of his torque. On the second stage, Stig broke a brake disc, and whilst he was having it changed at the end of that stage he watched Per have an accident on the third stage. Spectators had spread water at one corner in order to reduce the dust. Because of this Per lost the car's tail, the tail hit a tree and the car rolled three times, ending up rather flatter than anyone thought a Saab could end up. It took the fire brigade twenty minutes to get them out of the car. Luckily they were only slightly hurt. A bad 'yump' caused Stig to destroy his front shock-absorber mountings, but he still managed to come fourth. Simo spun and stalled on a late stage, so could only manage fifth. Rainio was seventh.

The official team for the RAC Rally consisted of Stig, Per and Tapio Rainio. Per spun on an early stage and then lost twelve minutes later when he rolled. Stig also rolled, but only lost four minutes—he then ran so short of petrol that he had to beg some from a marshal. All the cars were having problems with the brakes, but these were sorted out at Edinburgh. Per was doing very well but on the last stage broke a drive shaft and had to retire. Stig was also doing very well until he spun on an ice patch and broke his back axle which took fifty minutes to repair. This put him down to second position, and Rainio was thirteenth. Saab were also first and second overall in the Jemt Rally.

Changes for 1975

The new grille on the Combi—made of the same materials as that on the 95/96, and with the outline of the Saab grille wider and slightly shallower—was extended to all the 99 models in 1975. The EMS was slightly different in having a second line tracing the grille frame within the main one. The badge on the rear of the EMS was also new. At the other end of the scale the designation X7 had been dropped and the least expensive car was just called the 99. The car was given the same bumpers and wheels of the rest of the range and the two litre engine—the 1·85 litre engine therefore having been dropped from all models. The petrol tank was increased by 2·1 gallons to 12 gallons on all saloons to bring them in line with the Combi. The brakes were slightly modified and received a larger vacuum servo. The steering wheel was also changed and the drive shaft strengthened. A more durable exhaust system was fitted. Saab had always had some problems of reliability with the complex Bosch Jetronic system, a very good system when it was working. So they changed over to the Bosch constant-injection mechanical system, which proved just as efficient as the Jetronic system but significantly more reliable. The 95/96 models for 1975 looked very little changed from the previous year's 95 and 96, though the windscreen wipers were painted black to avoid glare. In fact a very important change had taken place: for some years the gearbox had caused problems. It had always been the car's weakest link and as time went on it was becoming increasingly obvious that something needed to be done. A new gearbox casing had been tested in the rally V4s and had proved successful, so was introduced to the production model and was largely successful in curing the gearbox problem.

As Saabs had been manufactured for twenty-five years it was decided to produce a Silver Anniversary model of the 96. The car was painted in silver crystal with lion-yellow upholstery. The grille and rear extractor covers were matt black, and a matt-black and chrome strip was fitted below the side windows. Ornate wheel embellishers were fitted. The car was only available on certain markets, 150 being exported to Britain, and each car had an individual numbered plaque. Assembly of the 95 was moved from Trollhattan to Arlov.

In February 1975 a new engine was added to the 99 range. It had twin Stromberg 150 CD carburettors and produced 108 bhp, 8 bhp more than the single-carburettor engine and 10 bhp less than the European versions of the petrol-injection engines. To begin with, this engine was fitted to the European versions of the Combi, but was soon extended to other selected models in the range.

The 1975 Rally Season

In the 1975 Arctic Rally Stig was fastest in thirty-four of the forty-five stages, but he also went off the road once or twice and so had to fight hard to get second place. Simo drove brilliantly and came first. His team mate Jari Vilkas was third. In the Canadian Winter Rally a Saab came fifth, another had been fifth before this one, but had retired halfway when the engine blew up. In the Swedish, Stig was morally second, though actually third. The rally was hard fought between the Saabs and the Lancia Stratos, with Stig being in the lead for most of the rally, and Per in third place. Stig drove very well, winning twenty-six out of thirty-six stages. Unfortunately, because of an electrical fault his engine died and he had to be pushed over the line by Per—this put him into second position and Per into fourth. He was then given a 500 sec penalty for not finishing the rally under his own power, which put him down to third position.

In two of the rallies in the Scottish championship Alistair Robertson finished sixth and ninth. In the Elba, Stig took the lead from the start, but on the third and fourth stages, which were tarmac, he dropped back to sixth. He later retired with gearbox failure. In the

Nordland Rally, Stig drove a 99 on its first official rally outing. However the car's engine was somewhat difficult to keep running— it had to be push-started from the start of stage three. Then there was the unfortunate incident on one stage where the rally had to cross a main road which had not been closed off. Stig missed an arrow and turned down the main road instead. Ultimately it was the engine of the car that forced him to retire when it failed completely.

Stig made a very good start in the 1,000 Lakes, rather too good, as on Stage 11, when lying third, he was clocked doing 73 kph in a 60 kph limit and was disqualified. Simo drove perfectly, but was beaten into second place by Mikkola because a metal fragment from the air cleaner drew itself into an inlet pipe and caused the car to misfire on one cylinder. Per was pushing Makinen hard all the way, but could not quite catch him, and so came fourth. Tapio Rainio's fuel-injection car had the engine seize because the cylinder head had been imperfectly machined. J. Vilkas came seventh and another Saab was tenth.

Both Stig and Per had cars in the RAC Rally, and started very well—at the end of the first stage they were lying first and second. Per retired later that first day with engine failure. Stig stayed in the lead until the sixteenth stage, when Makinen took over. Stig was pulling back well, but was put out by crankshaft failure.

Changes for 1976

The 1976 model was no longer called merely '95' or '96', but the '95L' and the '96L' to parallel the 99 designations. The most obvious difference was the fitment of the 99 impact-absorbing bumpers to both models. This completely changed the image of the cars: whilst the practicality of the new bumpers is undeniable, it might be said that they made the cars look heavy, particularly at the rear of the 95, where the number plate had to be moved up on to the tail gate and flanked by two large black lamps. Inside, the cars had the speedo-meter and the instrument containing the temperature gauge and the fuel gauge from the 99, and the 99's steering wheel with the larger padded centre. The seating arrangement had been subtly redesigned so that the rear-seat passengers had more leg room. This was particularly true for the 95, because the spare wheel had been moved from its traditional position under the rear seat and had been put under the boot floor in a similar manner to the 96 spare wheel. This meant that the third row of seats had been done away with and the 95 had become only a five-seater. One of the major reasons for this was the worry about the safety aspect of the third row of seats—in a rear end collision the occupants of these seats ran the risk of very serious injury, particularly to their legs and to their necks, since it was not possible for head restraints to be fitted. From that point of view the deletion of the third row of seats was a good thing, but it did make the car significantly less practical and probably represented the final blow for the 95 as it was no longer as competitive as it had been on the export markets. The suspension settings for both 95 and 96 were altered slightly, and the 96 was given wider wheels. The choke was no longer of the automatic type, a significant advance.

On certain markets, the 99 base model became known as the 99L, and the 99L became known as the 99GL. It was not until the Brussels Motor Show in January 1976 that the really interesting new models were announced. The real new model was the five-door Combi Coupe. Obviously Saab had been influenced by the success of the three-door Combi, the formula they used being the same. The roofline of the car was exactly the same as the four-door model, and the tail treatment the same as the three-door Combi. Of course Saab could not change the rear side window because it was incorporated in the door, but they were faced with a considerable problem as the new tail left a large area of blank metal behind the rear door. This was bad for visibility and made the rear seat dark and looked a trifle strange. So, what became known as an 'opera window' was fitted to the car. This in itself made the car look distinctive, though its looks were not to everyone's taste. The car was certainly practical and continued Saab's progress up-market, confirming adherence to the hatchback concept. It was initially made part of the GL range.

The other new model was based on the four-door saloon. Saab considered that a four-door saloon with petrol injection and an automatic gearbox would be a very good seller—of course they already had a model of this type in their L range, but a lot of potential buyers probably did not realise this. Saab's other problem centred around the EMS—as it was their only top-of-the-range model, they could not make it as sporting as they might have wished as it had to have wide appeal. A lot of people wanted a car with trim like the EMS, but with four doors. So from these requirements a new model was developed, the GLE. It had four doors, petrol injection and was available only with an automatic gearbox. The exterior and interior trim were similar to that of the EMS, in some cases rather better—the new car had rear-seat headrests and the areas of the alloy wheels finished in black on the EMS were finished in gold on the GLE. The door mirrors were adjusted electrically, and stereo speakers mounted in the doors. The glass was tinted all round, and the paint was a special metallic, usually charcoal grey. Undoubtedly it was a very civilised motor car. Many would have liked to have seen one with a manual gearbox, but the theory was that if you wanted a manual transmission you probably would also want the extra sportiness of the EMS. The EMS itself changed somewhat with the introduction of the GLE: the springs were made stiffer, Bilstein shock absorbers were fitted and rather a large front spoiler was added. The steering ratio was altered to make it more responsive. The rest of the 99 saloons were fitted with new hub caps without Saab motifs on them. January 1976 was a significant month for Saab in another way too as it was the month during which the millionth Saab rolled off the production line.

The 1976 Rally Season

In the Arctic there were no Swedish official Saabs, only Finnish. All were 1815 cc cars, Simo's being injection and the other two, Tapio Rainio and Jari Vilkas, having carburettor cars. Simo took an early lead, but a cracked gearbox casing allowed the differential to come out of mesh and he had no choice but retirement. Tapio therefore took over the lead, with Jari second. Unfortunately Jari put his car off the track and lost fifteen minutes trying to get it on again. When he put it off the track again, he retired. This left Tapio clear to take a good victory.

Boucles de Spa was the first outing for the EMS fitted with the 16 valve version of the engine, which is considered later. Stig gained a very easy victory with it, and the engine caused quite a stir. The Swedish was made especially interesting because it was the first time it was tackled without practice. Stig and Per were in works V4s, Johansson in an EMS entered by the Sport and Rally department. Naturally there were many private V4s entered, whose numbers were being swelled by an increasing number of private EMSs. Per led from the start, with Stig second. Early in the rally Erkki Temmes in a private V4 lost a rear wheel and spun to a halt. Dag Petersson in another private V4 lost all his petrol on stage seven when in sixth place. The rally became purely between Stig and Per, with Per in front. The snow was falling very heavily and it became more of a battle to dig the cars out fastest after a spin rather than a battle of fast driving. Kurt Malmgren, in a private EMS, put it so far into a snow drift that it could not be dug out. The rally ended with Per winning, just ahead of Stig in second place. Ulf Sundberg was fifth in an EMS and Gustafsson ninth in a 99.

There were no Swedish-entered works Saabs in the Hankiralli either, but Finnish ones for Simo and Tapio Rainio—injection— and a carburettor car for Jari Vilkas. Jari had rather bad luck and drove into a BMW after having been blinded by snow. He got going again, but retired after he went off the track again. Only a certain number of studded tyres were allowed per car. Tapio had conserved his studs in the early stages of the rally and was so able to pull away from the field at the end; Simo had not and so could not. Tapio was first, Simo third and another Saab seventh. Stig was driving a 16 valve EMS in the Welsh Rally, but after a promising start the car dropped a valve and he had to retire.

In the 1,000 Lakes Per and Stig had Swedish EMSs, whilst the Fins had V4s with transmission trouble, so much so that Simo opted for a car with an 1800 cc engine, rather than a 1900 cc one, in the hope of finishing the rally. Early on Stig bent his sump guard, which promptly smashed his sump (and smashed the distributor against the bonnet), causing him to retire. Per fared little better, breaking an oil pipe and having to retire with piston failure. Simo ran out of petrol and bought some from a farm—he soon found out that he had bought two-stroke mixture, so he had to go and find some more. He also had a leaking fuel pipe to the injector, which caused his car to misfire. Tapio Rainio lost eight minutes having a brake cylinder changed. Simo was fifth, Tapio seventh and Jari Vilkas eighth.

In the RAC Stig and Per were both in 16 valve EMSs. Stig drove steadily throughout, gradually moving up the placings. On the last morning he was lying second and poised to strike. However, on one stage he had two punctures on the same side of the car. He finished the stage, but had to continue on to the next stage without help from the service crew. He therefore put his one spare wheel on the front and continued rather more slowly, finishing second. Per had transmission trouble. He also hit a rock, bending a wheel—this was replaced, but a few stages had to be completed before the steering could be straightened out. He retired with differential failure. Saab gained the team prize with the help of a V4 and another EMS.

Changes for 1977

The most noticeable changes to the 99s for 1977 were the lights. The front indicators and sidelights were deepened so that they extended the whole depth of the grille—in contrast to the old lights most of the depth was taken up by the sidelights, to be used as day running lights on certain markets. The rear lights on the Combi remained the same but on the saloon they became considerably larger, over twice the size of the old ones. The bottom strip of the cluster was devoted to running lights and brake lights, while the top strip had a large area of indicator and reversing lights. The headlamps for 95/96 and 99 models were changed, a new design of improved dipped beam being less dazzling for drivers of oncoming cars. The 95 and 96 models were both fitted with electrically heated rear windows. The 96 received the front seats from the 99, the 95 not until some months afterwards. The rear seat of both models had already been somewhat modified. No such cars were exported to Britain. During the 1977 model year the output of the engine was increased by 3 bhp to 68 bhp by fitting a twin-choke carburettor. The capacity of the alternator was increased to 55 amps.

Turbo-Charging

With engine production moved from England to Sodertalje and Saab producing their own version, development work became much easier, and a lot of expert help became available from the Scania engineers. Turbo-charging was one of the ideas being experimented with and there was particular interest in BMW's experience with turbo-charging the 2002 in 1973. A great deal was learned from this and BMW's failure encouraged rather than provoked abandonment. The idea had great potential but BMW, in producing a car in almost racing trim, with the turbo tuned to give a high top speed and good acceleration at high speeds had gone about it in completely the wrong way. Saab therefore set about developing a turbo-charged version of the two litre engine which peaked at rather lower speeds and was usable within the normal rev range on the road. It was thought that a six- or eight-cylinder car was unnecessarily wasteful as the extra power accorded by it would be used perhaps 15 per cent of the time, whereas the extra petrol consumption would be present all the time. The first turbo-charged engines to be developed were V4s in 96 bodies to be used for rallycross. This proved to be fairly successful and so the decision was taken to go on with the development with the idea of producing a practical turbo-charged engine for the 99. Around this time Garrett, a US company, introduced a turbo-charger about the same size as an alternator. This seemed ideal for Saab's purposes but did pose a few problems. A small turbo-charger was needed to produce an acceptable amount of thrust at low gas-flow rates—in other words so that the turbo can cut in at low road speeds in the intermediate gears to give extra acceleration for overtaking. However, with such a turbo-charger, as speeds increased pressure would become too great. Conventional wisdom at that time dictated the use of a blow-off valve to lose this unwanted pressure. This idea did not appeal to Saab at all as they took the view that it was pointless to build up the pressure only to blow most of it off again. The other problem of a small turbo-charger is that it tends to cause back pressure, which quickly increases the temperature in the combustion chamber between the exhaust stroke and the next compression stroke. Saab therefore developed their own charging pressure valve, or wastegate. This enabled the turbo boost to be set at a fixed pressure. Up to that pressure the wastegate would remain closed, but once that pressure had been exceeded it would open, allowing enough exhaust pressure to bypass the turbine in order to reduce the pressure to its proper level. The rating of the wastegate could be simply altered to deal with changed pressure requirements for different fuel octanes or higher performance requirements. This idea was so original, and so effective, that Saab are patenting it.

The energy crisis of 1973 and 1974 convinced the engineers at Sodertalje that they were working along the right lines as they were obtaining a very satisfactory balance between performance and economy—after all when the engine was running under part load, perhaps 85 per cent of the time, it was no less economical than the normally aspirated injection unit. Most of the people at Nykoping were also convinced that the project had a future as it seemed to provide them with a very effective way of moving up-market, and changing the 99's rather staid public image. However, at Troll-hattan they were not too happy about the project and took quite a lot of convincing. It seems likely that they were worried that Saab might have a similar experience to BMW and not bounce back from it quite so successfully as BMW. However events were moving quickly. The market needed a more powerful Saab, particularly as there was a new range of cars on the way, and the market was reacting away from thirsty big-engined cars. The turbo seemed the ideal solution, and what's more, Saab did not seem to have much choice: if they wished to improve (or even merely consolidate) sales, they needed this, their only alternative.

The engine was very little changed for the turbo-charger. The block, the crankshaft, the bearings and the connecting rods were completely standard. New pistons had to be fitted to improve heat dissipation and to reduce the compression ratio from the standard figure of $9.2:1$ to $7.2:1$. The inlet valves were modified slightly and the exhaust valves given sodium cores to assist cooling. A milder camshaft was fitted to alter the timing. The radiator was enlarged, an oil cooler was fitted and the bore of the exhaust system enlarged. The primary reduction drive between the engine and the gearbox was fitted with a morse chain for extra strength and silent running. It is perhaps surprising to note that the sparking plugs were the same as those fitted to the standard 99. The engine included a number of safety devices to prevent its being damaged. Obviously the wastegate provides the first line of resistance but, in the event of this failing, a pressure switch cuts off the petrol temporarily. If the engine is over-revved a switch in the distributor will isolate the ignition until the revs fall below 6,000 rpm. To reduce engine wear the final-drive ratio was raised by about 10 per cent.

In its production form the engine produced 145 bhp at 5,000 rpm, against 118 bhp at 5,500 rpm for the normal injection engine before the fitment of the turbo. The BMW engine produced 170 bhp at 5,800 rpm. The Saab turbo produced 174 lb ft of torque at 3,000 rpm with a surprisingly flat torque curve. The standard engine produced 123 lb ft at 3,700 rpm and the BMW 177 lb ft at 4,000 rpm. The Saab turbo-charger begins to be felt at about 1,000 rpm, a remarkably low figure. At this point the turbo would be turning at about 10,000 rpm. At 3,500 rpm for the engine the turbine would be turning at about 50,000 rpm and its usable range extends up to about 80,000 rpm, though it can take up to 220,000 rpm without damage. The turbo-charging pressure is 0·7 bar.

The 99 Turbo

In September 1977 the Saab 99 Turbo was introduced in a Combi body (though the Combi Coupe designation was not applied to it). The car was equipped to a high level, similar to that of the EMS in suspension and the GLE in trim. What differentiated this car externally from its more lowly brethren was a rear spoiler below the rear window, rectangular driving lamps at the front and square fog lamps at the rear, and its own alloy wheels. Certainly their design was fresh and novel, and when they were moving they looked very effective, but when stationary they bore an uncanny resemblance to plastic wheeltrims. Inside, the car had a turbo gauge pod mounted on the top of the dash so that it would constantly be in the driver's vision. In Britain the car was basically only available in three-door form and painted black, though there was a limited edition of 100 five-door versions painted cardinal red metallic. To say that the car caused a considerable stir would be something of an understatement. It established Saab on the motoring map throughout the world and finally dispelled any lingering suggestion of staidness about Saab's image. The combination of five seats, large luggage capacity, good economy, a top speed of over 120 mph and fantastic acceleration finally convinced both journalists and public that Saabs were no longer things which you overtook to get away from the trail of blue smoke—indeed, Saabs had become things that you simply could not overtake. The new model received an excellent press and the demand for it was very high, far outstripping supply. The 1978 models of the other 99s were little changed, although the EMS and the GLE became available only in three- and five-door Combi form respectively. The Saab 99L had almost been phased out.

The 95L and 96L suddenly became the 95GL and the 96GL. They received front lamps and indicators on a par with those of the 99. The 96 received new rear lights which were an exercise in neatness: instead of curving around at the bottom, as they had always done, their inner edge followed the line of the bootlid, giving a larger area without spoiling the lines of the rear. A reversing light was also included in the cluster. Unfortunately Saab had become carried away with the idea of spoilers and were determined to fit one to the rear of the 96. Hence the old chrome boot handle was transformed into black thermoplastic and extended over the whole width of the boot—certain variants also had the area below the 'spoiler' painted matt black. Later cars were 'improved' by having their hub caps removed and 'go-faster' stripes added to the sides.

Exhaust-Emission Control

The two-litre engine has always been very clean in terms of emissions, particularly in its petrol-injection form. Until 1975 it had needed no modification at all to pass the US Federal and the Californian emission regulations. In 1975 the Californian regulations necessitated a little modification to the engine. It was given an air injection pump and the exhaust gases were partly recirculated. This dropped power to 110 bhp and obviously took the edge off performance. However, the loss was only slight. Saab were not very happy with this situation and so accelerated development on an alternative method of making the engine cleaner without running the risk of having to fit complex catalysts and thermal reactors for future legislation. They worked in conjunction with Bosch on this project and in 1977 the rather remarkable device called the Lamda sensor was announced. This was a ceramic plug inserted into the manifold to constantly monitor the air–fuel mixture and control the fuel injection. It was discovered that, if the air–fuel ratio was kept slightly leaner than the stoichio-metric figure of 14·5 the hydrocarbon and carbon monoxide levels decreased. With this fitted to the engine, only a three-way catalyst was needed to keep the Nox levels well down. Since 1977 this device has therefore been fitted to cars destined for the North American market. Though at the moment power output is little different from the old system of air pump and exhaust recirculation, the idea has great potential. On certain markets a deceleration valve is fitted to ensure that the excess fuel supplied when the acceleration is released is burnt efficiently. Cars with automatic transmission require an exhaust-gas recirculation device.

Into the Executive-Car Market: the 900

At the Paris Motor Show in October 1978 a new range of Saabs was introduced. Saab wanted to move positively into the executive-car market, rather than merely to hover on the fringe of it, and so they wished to produce a slightly larger car. For reasons of cost they could not afford to design a completely new car and, anyway, the 99 was still very competitive and remained superior to many younger designs. Hence, the decision was made to build a new car around the 99 which retained most of its features but was obviously different. It was decided to use the Combi Coupe versions of the car as a base for the new project as they were Saab's newest and most successful designs, and the top models of the 99 range were all Combis. The easiest way to increase the size of the car is to increase the front and rear over-hangs. This is of rather limited practical use as it would not have increased the usable interior space as that would still have been limited by the intrusion of the wheel arches. For this reason it was decided that the whole floorpan should be redesigned and the wheel-base should be increased from the 2,473 mm of the 99 to 2,525 mm. The main reason for lengthening was to provide extra space in the passenger compartment. This came with moving the front wheel arch forward. The body was 210 mm longer overall than the 99 Combi, 60 mm of this resulting from the larger bumpers and the remainder from the lengthening of the body. The front overhang was lengthened by 70 mm, 50 mm having been added between the engine and the firewall. The front was not merely lengthened, but redesigned as well. In order to save weight many of the steel members on the 99 were aluminium on the 900, such as the longitudinal members under the gearbox. Completely new steel structures were included to meet the latest US safety regulations—other structures had to be strengthened. It is interesting to note that the wheel arches and wing flanges were actually weakened so that they would collapse in the event of an accident and the doors could still be opened.

Steering was still similar to that of the 99, with a rack-and-pinion system, the box being set far back. The column had three universal joints in it so that the steering box could move backwards in the event of an accident without transmitting the force upwards through the steering column. At the top of the column was a pierced metal cowl which, in the event of a very serious accident, would deform in the safest possible way. The steering wheel centre was the safest built by Saab. It consisted of a lightweight deformable metal frame, on which a plastic pressure-distribution box was mounted. Covering the whole structure was a pad of soft plastic. There can be little doubt that this system is the safest on any production car in the world as it allows the driver to maintain control over the steering for an almost unprecedented length of time, and it is actually safer in the event of an accident to hit the steering column than anything else on the 900.

The safety of the steering was complemented by the redesigned suspension geometry. Obviously the suspension was on the same principle as that of the 99. Indeed at first glance the two systems seem little different. The front track of the 900 is 20 mm wider than that of the 99, and the travel of the front springs is 20 mm greater than that of the 99. Hence the risk of wheelspin has been reduced, this being particularly important on the Turbo models. The new geometries give improved anti-roll resistance without the need for an anti-roll bar. The rigid rear axle is 10 mm wider than on the 99, also rather stronger and heavier. The idea was that the rear of the car would be completely neutral and not exhibit any undesirable steering characteristics. The axle would also act as its own anti-roll bar as it twists under the load. The rear track is unaffected by variations of load as the axle is mounted below the wheel centres. In all, the suspension is rather better than the excellent system on the 99. Stability was further improved by the fitment of Michelin TRX and Pirelli P6 tyres to the five- and three-door Turbo models respectively.

One criticism of the 99, particularly the early models, was that the steering was excessively heavy at low speeds. Saab took this to heart and the steering mechanism of the 900 was completely new—an advanced US system manufactured by Saginaw, with Saab's own power assistance fitted to certain models. Both the steering and the power assistance seem to have won almost universal acclaim.

Saab's steering geometry incorporates rather a controversial principle. The steering radius is decided by the relative positions of the outer points of the upper and lower wishbones. Three different arrangements are possible: negative, neutral and positive. In the event of, for example, a tyre bursting at the front of the car negative geometry will compensate for the deviation of the car from its path, hence moving it back towards its original course. Neutral geometry will not affect the course at all, whilst positive geometry will emphasise any deviation. Conventional wisdom (Ford etc) states that negative geometry is best as the car will correct itself. However Saab have opted for positive geometry and justify it in this way: the driver of a car in the situation of a blow-out will tend to immediately try to compensate and steer the car back on to its original course. However, with negative offset steering, the car will supply him with confusing information as the steering wheel will move in the opposite direction to that of the car's pull. Thus the driver will try to correct the steering wheel and move it the wrong way—assisting the car to move off course. Neutral offset is almost as bad, as it offers the driver no information through the steering wheel and the driver has to rely on his senses. With positive offset the steering wheel moves in the same direction as the car's deviation, therefore supplying the correct information to the driver and enabling his initial reaction to be the correct one. For this reason a little positive offset is built into the 900's steering. The test of driving over a knife blade to slice one front tyre at about 60 mph and then braking to a halt without the driver's hands on the steering wheel displays not only the intrinsic stability of the car, but also how little positive offset is built into it.

The dashboard was completely new, and just as much of an advance as the remodelled dash had been in the 99. It was divided into two sections, the section for the driver taking up over half the width and curving slightly to make all the controls face him. The actual instruments were placed directly in front, a rectangular section having been removed for them. In the current fashion they were placed underneath a piece of non-reflective transparent material and deeply recessed to avoid glare. All cars had a large speedometer centrally positioned; the lesser models had this flanked on the left by a slightly smaller clock and on the right by a combination gauge of a similar type to the one used in the 99. On the EMS and the Turbo the left-hand gauge was a tachometer with a small clock at the bottom, and on the Turbo the right-hand gauge was divided into three sections and included a turbo-charger pressure gauge. Naturally a full range of hazard-warning lights were included. The lighting for the instruments was green, it being decided that this was the most restful of all possible colours and least likely to interfere with the hazard-warning lights. To the right of the instruments were the heating and ventilation controls. There can be no doubt that these are both supremely logical once understood and supremely confusing before. They consist of three circular controls: one for fan speeds; one for temperature control; and one for controlling which outlet the air comes from—this gives you six basic choices, before the controls on each individual outlet. However, once the basics are grasped the system is probably the best in the world. When getting into a cold car the driver will probably turn to setting one and as the car warms up gradually move through the settings until setting seven —complete shut-off is reached (this setting is also useful in cases of nuclear fallout). The system is the only one in the world to include a filter to remove pollen in the air and help hay-fever sufferers. It is made of oil-impregnated glassfibre and also removes from the air particles bigger than 0·002 mm, oil and soot, certain bacteria and certain heavy metals. Hence the interior of the car is more pleasant and the insides of the windows keep cleaner. Above the heater controls was a space for a radio, and below were the controls for heated rear window, hazard-warning lights and the like. To the right of the dashboard was a glove compartment, so designed that the driver could not reach it with the car in motion. The car had the normal twin steering-column stalks. The whole system is a paragon of ergonomic virtues. In true Saab tradition it is made of cellular plastic on a light steel frame with carefully calculated deformation properties, impacts on the passengers' thighs being reduced by specially padded knee-protection members below the dashboard.

The 900 had a new braking system with semi-metallic outer brake pads fitted, although semi-metallic inner brake pads could not be fitted because of the problem of heat build-up. Some of the wheels were new—the three-door Turbo and the EMS retained the same wheels. The standard steel wheels on the GL became somewhat sculpted, having triangular cooling slots and rather smaller centre discs. The GLE lost its alloy wheels and got large hub caps with a sort of broad spoke effect on them—very odd. The five-door Turbo got alloy wheels with a fine spoked effect and small centre discs. Many details of the car were different from those on the 99. The wipers were asymmetrical to give a better field of vision and to reduce the distraction for the driver of the passenger-side wiper passing into his vision. Cooling capacity was increased by an improved radiator and a new water pump. On some markets a second electric fan was fitted to the car. Engine mountings were new, as were the electrics.

Of course the most noticeable thing about the car was the longer nose. This changed the balance of the car completely: the Combi Coupe with the 99 nose had always looked slightly strange, especially the five-door version. However, the new version looked far sleeker and more in keeping with the market for which it was aimed. It must be remembered that the top models had to be competitive with such cars as the Rover, the Citroen CX and all the other expensive executive saloons of Europe. The treatment around the front lights was much better: the sidelights and indicators were much bigger and faired into the body rather than standing proud of it. The headlamps for America were of course sealed-beam units, but rectangular, so for the first time in some years European and American Saabs looked pretty much the same. The European Saabs retained their non-sealed units, but the new ones were 30 per cent larger than those of the 99. In addition to this, the condensation trap had been improved, so the reflectors were less likely to corrode. A new grille was fitted to all models: the GL and GLE models had horizontally divided grilles with small Saab 'grille' outlines in the centre of them. The EMS and the two Turbo models had three bold vertical slots at each end of the grille with a plain area in the centre that suggested a traditional Saab 'grille'.

Not enough people realised that this was rather a different car from the 99. However, enough people did recognise it for a very good car for demand to far outstrip supply, even though prices were higher than the equivalent 99s had been. What was even more gratifying was that the greatest demand was for the top-of-the-range models, and the Turbo in particular. Saab's marketing gamble of moving into a very competitive section of the market with a rather unconventional car had obviously paid off very well indeed. Stories abound in marketing circles about Rolls-Royces and almost new Jaguar XJSs being traded in for new Saab Turbos. It would appear that Saab had moved into the right section of the market at the right time, and Saab virtues had at last been recognised by the car-buying public.

With the arrival of the 900 all the 99s were dropped except two models—the 99GL two- and four-door saloons, which were cheaper than any of the 900s and did not duplicate any model in the range. For 1979 the 99 was given the same front springs as the 900, and the rear axle was strengthened. It also had the 900GL wheels and seats.

For 1980 the 900 range received new front seats. Market resistance in Britain had always been strong to the high-back seat in the 99 and 900, so the new front seats had lower backs, but improved support with an adjustable head restraint. The complete seat had been redesigned, the seat being rather deeper dished and the lumbar support firmer. As well as being safer and more comfortable, the seats were rather better looking. All the 99 and 900 models were fitted with them, but not the 96. New rear-light clusters were fitted to 99 and 900—new, of course, meaning bigger. On most markets they included motorway fog-warning lights. On markets where these lights were not allowed they just had enormous brake lights. On all models except the 96 (except those in the U.K.), a new 'space-saver' spare wheel was used, this weighed 6 kg less than the conventional spare, and took up less room in the boot—speed was limited to 80 kph with this wheel in use. The radiator grille used on the Turbo model was standardised across the range—this was a somewhat controversial move, as certain people thought that it might be better to keep the signs of model differences. There were certain gearbox changes throughout the range. A five-speed gearbox was made optional on the Turbo models and the EMS. The fifth gear was virtually an overdrive, so it made for smoother and more economic cruising. Bottom gear was made higher in ratio than before, to help cara-vanners. The GLE was offered for the first time with a manual gearbox as an option. The pressure for the addition of a manual gearbox came mainly from America, where, it was discovered, they wanted 'four on the floor' on their expensive imports, having all the automatics they could want from Detroit. A highly desirable new model had been added to the 99 range—a two-door Turbo. This was definitely a car of sporting pretensions, lighter and with better weight distribution than either the old three-door 99 or the 900. The car was produced so that Saab could continue their tradition of always rallying a car from their current range rather than a special.

The 900 range has also received a new model. The four-door saloon—available initially only in Turbo form—follows the market trend back to conventionally booted saloons. The car was designed by Bjorn Envall, and features a tail significantly different from that of the 99 saloon. The saloon was introduced in March 1980, at the Geneva Show, and made available in October, 1980.

Other Engine Projects

For some time Saab have been working on a high-compression engine. Conventional wisdom states that raising the compression ratio of an engine means more power but greater fuel consumption and worse emissions. Saab, in co-operation with Ricardo, increased the compression ratio of a two-litre engine to 11:1 and at the same time reduced the power of the engine by fitting a single 150CD carburretor, instead of the more normal twin 150CD carburettors. More important perhaps was the discovery that because the engine ran cooler the exhaust was also cooler and so the Nox gases were down, and because of the high turbulence of the inlet manifold the car needed no choke. The hydrocarbon and carbon monoxide levels are relatively low with a cold engine—though they are relatively high when the engine warms up. However, when the emissions are measured on the constant-volume sampling cycle the effect is favourable. There can be no doubt that Saab are pleased with the results of this project and it would be very surprising if some positive results were not seen in production models before too long.

Saab's other recent engine project was rather different in aim from the high-compression engine. The 16-valve engine was purely for competition work. It was obviously inspired by the Triumph Dolomite Sprint engine, though the engine had nothing else in common with the Sprint's. Work began in June 1975. The aim was to have the engine ready as quickly as possible, so the bottom end was left standard—in the same way as the turbo engine had been. Two cylinder heads were considered for the engine—one designed and produced by the English firm of Westlake, and the other designed by Axelsson. The Westlake head was considered to be very good but too expensive to produce and therefore the Axelsson head was used. In fact it was almost as good. The head was produced in two sections, the top half being purely devoted to the camshafts—two of them. The engine was tried both with twin 48 DCOE Webers and Lucas fuel injection, the Lucas system producing slightly higher outputs. With the Webers the engine produced 220 bhp at 7,500 rpm and 159 lb ft of torque at 5,500 rpm. However much the figures may belie it, it was a surprisingly tractable unit. The engine was very extensively bench-tested, and throughout all these tests the only problem was that one engine broke a connecting rod. The engine was tuned to 235 bhp and remained just as reliable—with its rev range extended quite safely to over 9,000 rpm. A hundred of these engines were built so that they could be homologated—sadly they lasted only a season because of a change in regulations. There were tentative plans to produce a limited edition of twin-cam cars, perhaps 400, for sale to the public. Indeed, it would seem that the engine in a slightly milder state of tune would have proved ideal for the EMS. However, it is probable that the success of the Turbo has killed off any plans and the engine will remain a museum piece.

Rallying: a Change of Policy?

Bo Swaner—the team manager—has adopted a very selective approach to rallies in the past couple of years. No longer can works Saabs be seen in virtually all the major events as was the case in the 1960s. Rallying has become a far more serious and expensive business. In 1977 there were, as had become normal, no works cars in the Monte Carlo, the early rallies being confined to Scandinavia. Stig won the Arctic Rally, the Swedish and the Bergslags in the 16-valve EMS which had made such a successful debut in 1976. The Rally of the 1,000 Lakes was slightly less fruitful. Stig Blomqvist, Per

Eklund, Tapio Rainio and Simo Lampinen were all entered in EMSs—but all failed to finish. Small comfort was the vast number of privately entered 96s still to be seen competing. In the Canadian Rally J.-P. Perusse was 5th in an EMS. In the RAC Stig and Per had works 16-valve EMSs and were going very well but unfortunately Stig was forced to retire. Per finished 9th overall.

In the 1978 Swedish Per was going very well in an EMS when he was forced to retire with a broken con rod. Stig took advantage of the Lancia–Saab agreement and drove a Lancia Stratos. Ola Stromberg came 9th in a 96. Stig was entered in the Criterium de Quebec (Canadian) in a 99 fitted with a Group 2 engine. Unfortunately it proved to be troublesome from the start—having to be rebuilt at the last minute when it was discovered that a crankshaft weight fouled a piston. The engine was down on power from the start but Stig's early retirement was caused by primary-gear failure. Two Group 1 cars were driven by Walter Boyce and Hendrik Blok, both cursed by brake trouble caused by the unprotected rear-brake callipers being worn away by stones. Blok's car came 8th overall and Boyce's car 10th. The RAC saw the first major appearance of the works turbocharged cars. Saab largely saw it as a testing ground. The cars ran well, after an early worry when Stig's fuel pump failed on the first stage. However, on stage 20, Stig had drive-shaft failure which virtually put him out of the rally. Per was put out on stage 22 with the same trouble. This proved a great disappointment for the team as no drive-shaft problems had been encountered in testing.

Saab had an excellent start to 1979 with Stig in a two-door Turbo driving superbly and winning the Swedish Rally. Per was less fortunate in his three-door car, as because of a fractured pressure pipe his turbo-charger gave constant trouble and forced him to retire. The Mintex Rally provided the Saab Dealers' Team with its first outing in the Sedan Open Championship. Stig came in a three-door Turbo to compete in this very snowy event. He had a very good drive in conditions which suited both him and the car and came first by a good margin. Second was Per driving a TR7 V8 for the British Leyland team. Stig was less fortunate in the Circuit of Ireland. Early in the rally he was slowed by the brake pads which were of the wrong type and literally melted. This meant that Stig drove much of the rally with virtually no brakes and that many sets of pads (and discs) were fitted to the car. Stig came overall 6th, a very good result considering the brake problems and Saabs being not altogether suited to tarmac rallies. In the Welsh Rally Stig was in second place in the early stages. Unfortunately a series of punctures lost him a lot of time and he had to be content with eighth. Punctures also lost him time in the Scottish Rally, as did the replacing of an overheated turbo-charger. He came seventh overall.

The question has been raised as to whether Saab will continue rallying. It is argued that many Saab customers today are not really very interested in rallying—as they were in the early 1960s. In addition the 900 is a large, heavy car with a considerable front overhang—not obviously a suitable car. The budget for rallying is reviewed annually and must justify itself. Probably at the moment its greatest justification is as a testbed for the car, and whilst the car keeps putting up good performances Saab rallying will continue.

6 The Saab Organisation Today

Saab–Scania is Sweden's largest organisation for advanced technological development. In terms of turnover it is the country's second largest industrial enterprise. This seems quite a step from the small, and relatively young, aircraft company that decided to diversify into motor-car production to try to widen a narrow product base. Organisationally, the company is divided into four product divisions: Aerospace, Saab cars, Scania trucks and Nordarmatur. In addition to this there is the slightly mysterious 'Other activities', which in fact turns out to include military and civil electronics, equipment for steam and heat production and similar interesting—and often pioneering—engineering projects.

To examine the future of Saab cars, it is also necessary to look at the present and future activities of the whole of the Saab–Scania group, as it is no longer possible to look upon any one division as a financial island. The Aerospace division looks to have a fairly bright future, with the Viggen combat and fighter aircraft considered one of the best aircraft of its type in the world, and with Saab's policy of continuous development rather than radical change it should remain the mainstay of the Aerospace division until well into the 1980s. This is not to say that they are resting on their laurels: a light attack and training aircraft known as the BL3A is being developed. This anticipates a movement away from large and expensive aircraft to the smaller and relatively less expensive. The new aircraft incorporates a number of novel solutions to the problems of aircraft design. For instance the majority of the plane will be built out of carbon fibre reinforced plastics, thus reconciling the conflicting needs for great strength and light weight. Perhaps this technology will provide a useful spin-off in the field of car production where strength and

144

light weight are also becoming increasingly important. Aerospace
also produce a range of missiles and target systems. Not surprisingly
they are Sweden's largest defence contractor. However, this, their
greatest asset, also highlights their greatest weakness. They are
almost totally reliant on the Swedish government's defence policy
for their survival. Although they would be hard put to find a better
customer, it is still unwise for any company to be so committed to
a single buyer. Saab Aerospace recognise this and would like to
expand into civil aircraft again, though the cost involved in developing the aircraft and the near saturation of this particular market
sector tend to throw doubts upon the feasibility of any such projects.
The Aerospace division are also working on other projects not
directly connected with aircraft: the 'Saab Sub', an underwater
robot designed to work on the sea bed, for instance. In addition to
this there is the wind-powered generator project. At present tests of
a prototype generator with a turbine of 18 metres diameter are
proving so successful that full-scale prototypes with turbine diameters
of 50 metres or more are being planned. This important project
perhaps gives us a glimpse of the expanding role of the Aerospace
division.

The Scania division now has a wide range of good quality trucks
well known for their durability and their high earnings factors. It is
by some margin the largest division within Saab–Scania, having the
largest number of employees and the highest turnover, and with
about 85 per cent of its products going for export it is also a useful
source of foreign exchange. It would seem likely that Scania's future
will be fairly bright, as they seem to be working along the right lines
with their constant development in the fields of increased safety, with
work on such projects as seize-free braking systems and the like. They
are also working to make their vehicles more economical with
improved combustion and altered gearing. Of course Scania's future
is very much linked to the future of the whole heavy-road-transport
industry, which in the long run looks a little grim, because of con-
siderations of environment and energy. However, Scania would
seem to have sufficient flexibility, both from their relatively small
size and their innovative skill, to ride such economic storms rather
better than most of their rivals. Scania make an important contribution to Saab cars, in so much as they manufacture most of the engines
and all the gearboxes. It is interesting to note that Scania market

Volkswagen, Audi and Porsche cars and light commercials in Sweden—a hangover from the old pre-Saab–Scania days.

The Nordarmatur division manufacture valves and complete piping systems. They have such a wide range of systems that their future is assured, especially as they are working with Datasaab to produce computerised systems. Datasaab is a joint project between Saab–Scania and the Swedish government to develop computerised business and terminal systems. Significant progress is being made in this relatively new sector of operations, and it seems a sector with considerable scope for expansion and diversification. Indeed, an automatic board trimmer for sawmills has been successfully developed and installed, and series deliveries have already been started. Other applications, such as security systems, and military training and control systems are also progressing well. Saab have a partnership with the Sperry Rand Corporation marketing computers in Scandinavia. Saab–Scania are also involved in the manufacture of machine tools, textile process equipment, 'all-fuels' boilers and have just introduced on to the Nordic market an adaptation of an American solar-heating system.

It seems that the Saab–Scania group of companies is a very stable organisation economically, and it looks as if it will continue to prosper in the foreseeable future. The car division successfully rode out the economic storms of the middle 1970s—probably rather better than the rest of the motor industry. They have a very good range of cars in the 900—particularly the Turbo models of the range—and these cars should remain competitive into the late 1980s, perhaps longer. However, Saab, like any other small motor manufacturer, are conscious of the great expense of developing a completely new model. It was really for this reason that talks started between Volvo and Saab in 1976 about possible merger plans—the present range of Volvos being sorely in need of replacement. To begin with, the Saab board were in favour of the plan, but as negotiations continued they began to lose their enthusiasm. It was thought that Volvo, as the larger company, would become dominant in any partnership, Saab quickly losing its identity. The two companies were essentially incompatible because of their differing approach to cars.

The important partnership with Lancia began in a very low-key way. In 1975 it was thought that Saab might market a small car through their dealers. Many cars were looked at, and the one that

146

looked the most hopeful was the Italian Autobianchi. One was privately purchased and taken to Sweden to be studied in greater detail. The car was approved and a deal signed with Autobianchi which meant that Saab marketed Autobianchis in Sweden, Denmark, Norway and Switzerland. Unfortunately sales of the small car were not as good as expected. The car itself was good, but such small cars were not popular in Sweden. When Autobianchi were taken over by Lancia in 1976 Saab were having serious doubts about the partnership. What changed their minds was news of the new small Lancia which was at a late stage of development. A replacement was needed for the 95/96 range and this car seemed to have possibilities. Even coming in at such a late stage of the project Saab engineers were able to directly influence such things as the heating system, rust-proofing, the driver's seat and the tailgate opening. The car is now marketed by Saab in the above-mentioned countries as the Saab 600. So successful has this co-operation been that engineers from the two firms are working on a joint floorpan which should, some time in the late 1980s, provide a replacement for both the Saab 99/900 and the Lancia Beta. The two cars would have different bodies fitted on to them so that these two very individual companies will retain their identity.

In the shorter term work is being done on the turbo-charged engine. The problem of increasing performance by raising boost pressure is that the resulting increase in temperature increases the risk of pre-ignition. Hence Saab have developed a system of water injection. This injects a spray of water into each cylinder as soon as a certain temperature has been reached. The evaporation can lower the charge temperature by as much as 100°C. The system is at present producing 170 bhp at 5,500 rpm in a car referred to as the Saab Super Turbo 900. This car is also used to test suspension, wheels and spoilers. In addition it features a full-width rear fog light, cleverly mounted in the spoiler.

And what of other engines? Saab say they have no plans for fitting a diesel engine in the near future as they do not think that there is the demand for one and it would not fit their increasingly sporting image. This is probably true at the moment, but with the energy situation uncertain it must be hard to look far into the future. Saab have a version of their engine which runs on liquid petroleum gas—it has been tested in Stockholm taxis for some time. These tests have been generally successful, but Saab say that the decision as to whether they fit them into production models depends largely on whether the oil companies decide to market LPG widely or not. The electric-car project has now been shelved as insufficient progress was being made. The Finnish arm of the company is known for its unconventionality, and its innovative skill. Amongst other things it has produced long-wheelbase limousines. Naturally this can be of great help to the Swedish designers, though they have been known to rather embarrass the management (as in their recent marketing of a car running on paraffin).

It might be said that Saab have come a long way from the 92, and indeed the 96. Certainly many owners of older Saabs can no longer afford a new one. They have moved up in terms of market sector, but still provide the same combination of individuality and engineering quality that has been their hallmark from the start.

Appendix

The Sonnetts

On 16 March 1956 a new Saab, different from any other, was first seen at the Stockholm Motor Show. This was the Saab Sonett Super Sport. The big disappointment was that it was not for sale. Over 1955 and the early part of 1956 Rolf Mellde designed and built a light-weight sports car based on the 93. This was partly a personal project, and partly to prove to the world that Saab could produce a sports car. It seems probable that Saab had no intention of marketing such a car at that time, if only because they could sell as many saloons as they could make and did not really have the spare capacity to produce a low-volume sports car, which was not really suited to the home market. In addition it would have been very expensive to produce—being riveted aluminium throughout, though it must be said that the Americans would have liked a sports car to sell in order to capitalise on Saab's enviable reputation for handling and road-holding, and their growing competition record. One needs only to look at the sales of the MG TF in America to see that there was a considerable demand for a small sports car over there. So perhaps this car was more a means of sounding the market than Saab will admit. Rolf Mellde abandoned the floorpan of the 93 and designed his own chassis along aircraft principles. It was made of riveted aluminium with monoque construction based around box sections. This made it very strong and equally light. The body was fibreglass, and particularly light as the floorpan extended to form the bottom of the body, a louvered section along the side and the grille at the front. The rest of the body was simple and streamlined, with very large wheel arches to accommodate the standard 15 in diameter wheels. The car was purely a two-seater, and for a windscreen it had a low curved piece of perspex. The rest of the chassis components— steering, suspension and the like—were almost straight off the 93. The engine was of course the 748 cc unit, turned through 180° to improve the weight distribution, normally tuned to give about 57·5 bhp at 5,000 rpm. As the car weighed under 1,100 lb this gave very brisk performance, with a top speed of around 103 mph (rather than the 125 mph top speed that the US arm of the company attributed to it). The car was quite compact as well as light, with an overall length of only 138 in and a height of 32·5 in. It is interesting to note that the car was actually announced in the US, indeed two versions were announced: a competition version with special brakes and cooling system and one for personal use with a soft top and luggage compartment. It is a pity that no more than four were ever completed. Two more were never finished, but at least the project did show Saab that there was a ready market for their sports car, and that it was something to be borne in mind. Much of the work done in tuning the engine for the Sonett was carried over to the GT750.

In the early 1960s the Americans were pressing even harder for a sports car from Saab, and two design exercises were commissioned. The car had to be a closed sports coupe, stylish but cheap to produce. Sports-car prototype Number 1 was designed and made by Malmo Aircraft Industry, the actual designer Bjorn Karlstrom. He produced a neat fastback two-seat coupe with a flowing nose that ended in a single leading edge under which was the radiator air intake. The shortness of the car was emphasised by its very short rear overhang and 'sawn off' tail. The whole effect, while not elegant, was very pleasing. Sports-car prototype Number 2 was more of an in-house affair, being designed by Sixten Sason and constructed by ASJ. Sason took his normal strict utility approach to the design, using the complete floorpan and underbody structure of the 96—this may be seen in the use of the windscreen frame from that car. This, whilst being practical from a construction point of view, was unfortunate in terms of the car's styling as it made the car extremely high for a sports coupe. This was coupled with his desire to retain some form of marque identity so he built in a Saab-type grille and vestigial mouldings on the bonnet. All this gave the car a slightly strange appearance. Though it must be said that his version did have a number of very pleasing features such as a concave rear window and a removable targa top. For all this, it was Karlstrom's diminutive white car that was finally chosen in preference to Sason's slightly brash red one, although styling was not the only reason for the choice. Extensive comparative tests were done on the two cars, which showed the Sason car to have steering problems which would have been difficult to cure. The car made its first public appearance at the Hedenlunda Rally, a special press event, on 4 February 1965, though it was by no means in its final stage. By the spring of 1966 a prototype run of 24 cars had been built at the ASJ plant in Arlov, though in the end the cars were built at the MFI plant. These differed in detail from the original car. To begin with they were constructed of fibreglass (the original car had been constructed of steel in order that a fibreglass mould could be taken from it). The whole car looked less rounded—edges had been hardened and a 'crease' had been styled in between the wheel arches. The form of the grille had also been changed. Series production started at the end of 1966 and details had again been changed by then. The grille had changed from looking like an oval loudspeaker on a pre-war wireless to a much more acceptable series of horizontal slats. The car was given some proper front indicators and sidelights flanking the grille, rather than the tiny repeaters on the wings. The ventilation system was made 'flow-through'; the most obvious sign of this was the addition of 96-type extractor vents behind the side windows. The 'Triumph Herald type' bonnet catches were replaced by rubber toggles. The metal sport dash was replaced by a wooden dash into which the sport instruments were mounted. Less obvious was the improvement of the brakes. It is interesting to note that the car did not have any bumpers, merely a narrow rubber strip along the front leading edge and small rubber overriders at the back to protect the rear lights (which came from the 95). This car, the Sonett II, was probably the most sporting of all the production Sonetts. It had the Monte Carlo 850 engine which gave it 60 bhp. A triple-carburettor system was developed especially for the Sonett, and made it very well balanced, and quite suitable for competition. The car was involved in a certain amount of rally work in Europe, but as it only had mixed success and was destined almost exclusively for the US market, it was soon dropped in favour of the 96 body. The little car was quite a success in the US, although the two-stroke engine did rather limit its appeal. With this in mind, the Sonett in 1968 was fitted with a standard V4 engine producing 65 bhp. The car was no faster than the old two-stroke model, and as it was more nose-heavy it handled slightly less neatly. However, it could exceed 100 mph and was surprisingly economical, helped in these respects by a drag factor of only 0·32. In all, the car had been transformed from a competition car into a brisk grand tourer. It would have been impractical to race in V4 form as the engine capacity put it into a very competitive class. The other big improvement in the new model was that the column gearchange was moved to the floor and became commendably precise. Externally the V4 can be told from the two-stroke by a large bulge on the bonnet and rubber overriders at the front. It is interesting to note Saab's approach to the Sonett. The sales brochure outlined the performance of the car which, while very adequate for normal use, was rather limited if the car was viewed as a sports car in competition with such cars as Alfa Romeos. The brochure then outlined the safety features of the car—the primary safety of any Saab and a considerable amount of secondary safety too: all the cars had a proper roll bar behind the seats. The brochure then justified the car by asking if the potential owner really wanted more performance than 0–60 mph in 12·5 sec and a top speed of a little over 100 mph. Perhaps most revealing was the fact that the brochure asked people interested in the car to go to their Saab dealer and ask for the toy department. The car was a success, both in terms of sales and in terms of improved image. In all, 1,868 Sonett IIs were sold in the period up to 1969, 1,610 of them V4s.

At the end of the 1960s it was decided that the Sonett was beginning to look a trifle dated. Saab wanted something a little more up-market-looking to fit their new 99-based image, yet they did not wish to totally lose the shape of the Sonett II. A number of attempts were made to try to come up with a better design within the factory, but none was particularly successful, tending to be rather overstyled around the nose. One thing the design team were sure of—they wanted some form of tailgate, so the designs produced for the tail were more successful. It was decided to enlist the help of an Italian stylist, Sergio Coggiola. The final car had the same wheelbase as the old car but was 5 in longer in overall length at 154 in. The new car retained the line of the old one but looked altogether sleeker. The tail was of similar design but had a longer overhang, which made it look less 'abrupt'. Gone was the wrap-round rear window; in its place was a large flat pane which opened with an internal catch to give good access to the luggage compartment. It is interesting to note that the rear of the car was designed in Sweden rather than in Italy. The side of the cockpit looked different—the side window treatment was more in the style of the Sason prototype with the window in the door with a quarterlight and another small window behind the door. This left a blank area which emphasised the fastback styling of the car. The frontal treatment was a lot smoother: the nose was longer in front of the wheels and, instead of coming to an edge, ended in a narrow horizontal grille with a slightly raised centre section to denote Saab. A bulge, black-topped, graced the centre of the bonnet, and behind this was an air-scoop. At each end of the grille were small round sidelights, and under it a narrow rubber strip which acted as a bumper. The actual headlights were not visible, but concealed under flaps on the bonnet. This cleaned up frontal styling considerably, but as the headlamps had to be raised by a good hard tug on a manual control in the car rather than by an electric motor it must have been a bit of a nuisance, and made flashing impossible. The fascia on the Sonett III was new. It consisted of three circular dials mounted directly in front of the driver, the normal pair from the 95/96 plus a matching tachometer, the dials being quite heavily cowled. To the right of the dash was a lidded glove compartment, below which was a grab handle. In the centre of the dash was a dropped-down section, on which were mounted various switches, the heater controls and the ashtray. The whole dash was painted in a crackle-black finish. The short gear lever was mounted in a small centre console. The rest of the trim was generally simple, although not spartan. The seats did not recline, though they had an adjustment for lumbar support. Mechanically the III was the same as the 95/96, receiving the de-tuned 1·7 litre engine, a rather neat feature being the bracing tube across the engine compartment which doubled as an expansion tank for the cooling system. The car was altered slightly in 1972, receiving a black-plastic grille on very similar lines to those later received by the 99s. This suited the car very well and was complemented by the rear panel being painted black. The car was also given wider-base aluminium wheels, like those available as options on the 96, but without the black sections. This improved the look of the car and reduced the unsprung weight. The 1974 model had the bumpers from the 99 added to it to conform with US safety regulations. Whilst they hardly improved the appearance of the car, it wore them surprisingly well. It also had headlamp wipers.

The last year of production for the Sonett was 1974 as the next round of US emission regulations would have necessitated considerable redesigning of the car, and it simply was not considered worth it on such a low-volume car—a sad loss, but probably a wise commercial decision after 8,351 Sonett IIIs had been built. Drawings were made of a 99-engined Sonett, but it was never taken further.

There have of course been other 'sports' prototypes, the most notable one being the Formula Junior car which is dealt with elsewhere. In the early 1960s there were plans to build a two-seat convertible in Australia. This was quite a pleasantly styled car, though the only way you could tell that it was a Saab from its external appearance was by the size of the wheels. The car was to be built by a company called Lightburn & Co in Adelaide, but at an early stage in the plans it went bankrupt. In America it was recognised that the 850 cc engine was very suitable for powering sports/racing cars in the 850 cc class. One particularly successful car was produced in 1962 and called the 'Bobsy'. It must be said, though, that only the engine had anything to do with Saab. The US 'Quantum' was more serious than the Australian car. Although the two looked similar the 'Quantum' was less Saab-based, using a Saab engine, gearbox and certain other chassis components in rather a crude space frame. Parts had actually been bought from Saab to assemble some cars, but very little actually came of it.

Acknowledgements

I should like to express my thanks to John Edwards, Press and PR Manager for Saab (GB) and to his opposite number in Sweden, Peter Salzer. To Gunnar A. Sjögren of Marketing and Product Development for his invaluable help, and his line drawings. To Olle Lindkvist, Chief Testing Engineer, and Kjell Knutson, Manager of Car Function Testing, for their assistance on technical matters. To Torsten Åman for his help on rallying. Also to Hans Thornqvist, Public Relations Director.

Peter Brooke and his staff at the National Motor Museum Library for their patience and assistance with research on rallying; also David Tindsley for his help with that research. Paula Goldstein at *Motor Sport*, Tony Smith, Oliver Ryan, Jack Astley, Keith Wellington, Kevin Reade and Richard Kennedy.

Finally, my thanks to my mother, Barbara Chatterton, for so successfully performing the mammoth task of typing the manuscript, and to my father, Bruce Chatterton, for his assistance.

Index

157